*First published in Great Britain
in 1986 by Pavilion Books Limited
196 Shaftesbury Avenue, London WC2H 8JL
in association with Michael Joseph Limited
44 Bedford Square, London WC1B 3DU*

Distributed in the United States by Viking Penguin Inc

Text © 1986 Alan Hamilton

Designed by Bernard Higton

*Hamilton, Alan, 1943–
The Royal One Hundred
1. Royal house — Europe   2. Europe — Kings
and rulers — Genealogy
929.7'094   CS404*

*ISBN 0-907516-79-3
ISBN 0-907516-93-9 Paperback*

*Phototypeset by Tradespools Ltd., Frome, Somerset, England.
Printed and bound in Great Britain at Butler and Tanner.*

*ACKNOWLEDGEMENTS:
The author gratefully acknowledges particular assistance from the following
in the compilation of this book: His Majesty King Constantine of Greece;
Prince Tomislav of Yugoslavia; Ivan Bilibin; John Brooke-Little; Professor
Robin Medforth-Mills; Mrs Annemor Most; David Williamson.*

*The photographs in this book have been gathered from the following
sources:
Alexander of Yugoslavia, 106; Alpha/Jim Bennett 38; Her Highness the
Princess Astrid of Norway 92; Associated Press (left)/Anwar Hussein 30
(right); BBC Hulton Picture Library 6, 7, 99, 100, 107; His Imperial Highness
the Grand Duke Vladimir of Russia/Ivan Bilibin 123; Camera Press 13, 16, 17,
48, 74, 75, 102, 127; Peter Abbey 26, 67, Cecil Beaton 59 (left), Jim Bennett 33
(left), Anthony Crickmay 56, Alan Davison 45 (above right), Srjda Djukanovic
113, Dimitri Kasterine 55, 64, Patrick Lichfield 15, 23, 34 (far right), 40
(above), 60, David Linley 49, Norman Parkinson 35 (right), 42, 47, 50, Rude
86, Richard Slade 53, 110, 112, 114, Snowdon Cover, 15, 24, 27, 28, 36, 45; Deutsche
Presse 116; Mary Evans Picture Library 76; London Express 44; His Grace the
Duke of Fife 73 (left and right); Fox Photos 12; Tim Graham 21, 33 (above); D
Hudspeth 96; The Illustrated London News 35 (left), 41; Interfoto Archive 128;
Keystone Press Agency 62, 69; Knudsen Information a.s. 89 (right), 91 (right);
Robin Medforth-Mills 94, 103; Popperfoto 9, 77, 78, 80, 82, 85 (left and right),
89 (left), 91 (above), 98, 101, 105, 119; The Press Association Ltd 61, 65; Rex
Features Ltd 10, 52, 57, 118, 122; Spooner (Gamma)/ Bryn Cotton 37;
Syndication International 59 (right); John Topham Picture Library 18; Trond
S 83; Ullstein Bilderdienst 120, 126, 129; VG Photos 81, 87, 88; Collection
Viollet 121; Alan Warren 70.*

Illustration on back cover by Philip Argent

The Royal 100

A who's who of the first 100 people in line of succession to the British throne.

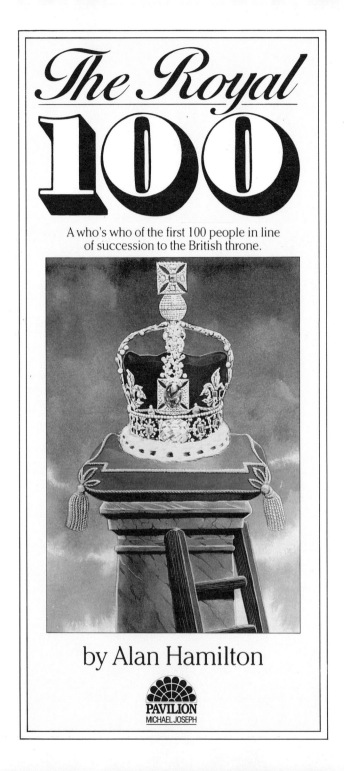

by Alan Hamilton

PAVILION
MICHAEL JOSEPH

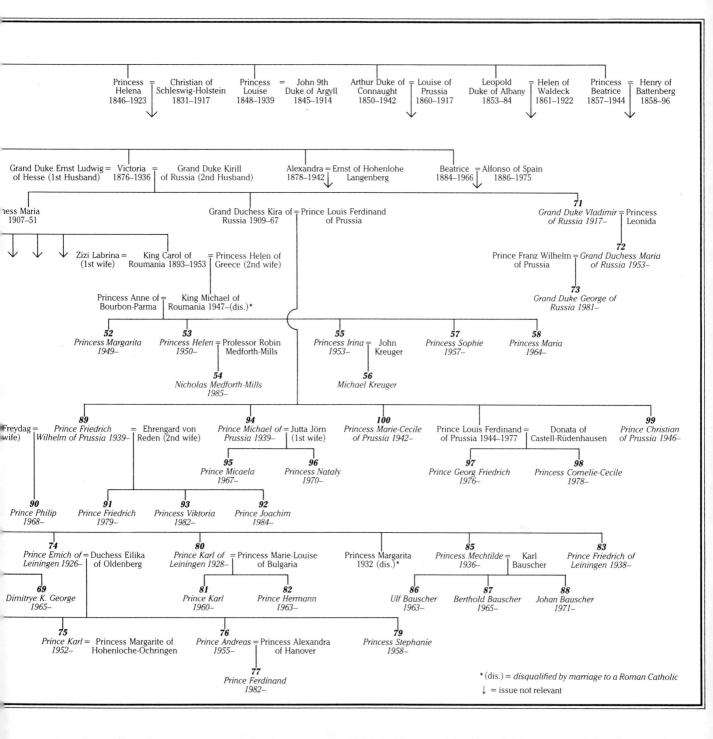

Princess Helena 1846–1923 = Christian of Schleswig-Holstein 1831–1917

Princess Louise 1848–1939 = John 9th Duke of Argyll 1845–1914

Arthur Duke of Connaught 1850–1942 = Louise of Prussia 1860–1917

Leopold Duke of Albany 1853–84 = Helen of Waldeck 1861–1922

Princess Beatrice 1857–1944 = Henry of Battenberg 1858–96

Grand Duke Ernst Ludwig of Hesse (1st Husband) = Victoria 1876–1936 = Grand Duke Kirill of Russia (2nd Husband)

Alexandra 1878–1942 = Ernst of Hohenlohe Langenberg

Beatrice 1884–1966 = Alfonso of Spain 1886–1975

71 *Grand Duke Vladimir of Russia 1917–* = Princess Leonida

ness Maria 1907–51

Grand Duchess Kira of Russia 1909–67 = Prince Louis Ferdinand of Prussia

72 Prince Franz Wilhelm of Prussia = *Grand Duchess Maria of Russia 1953–*

Zizi Labrina (1st wife) = King Carol of Roumania 1893–1953 = Princess Helen of Greece (2nd wife)

73 *Grand Duke George of Russia 1981–*

Princess Anne of Bourbon-Parma = King Michael of Roumania 1947–(dis.)*

52 *Princess Margarita 1949–*

53 *Princess Helen 1950–* = Professor Robin Medforth-Mills

55 *Princess Irina 1953–* = John Kreuger

57 *Princess Sophie 1957–*

58 *Princess Maria 1964–*

54 *Nicholas Medforth-Mills 1985–*

56 *Michael Kreuger*

Freydag = (wife) **89** *Prince Friedrich Wilhelm of Prussia 1939–* = Ehrengard von Reden (2nd wife)

94 *Prince Michael of Prussia 1939–* = Jutta Jörn (1st wife)

100 *Princess Marie-Cecile of Prussia 1942–*

Prince Louis Ferdinand of Prussia 1944–1977 = Donata of Castell-Rüdenhausen

99 *Prince Christian of Prussia 1946–*

95 *Prince Micaela 1967–*

96 *Princess Nataly 1970–*

97 *Prince Georg Friedrich 1976–*

98 *Princess Cornelie-Cecile 1978–*

90 *Prince Philip 1968–*

91 *Prince Friedrich 1979–*

93 *Princess Viktoria 1982–*

92 *Prince Joachim 1984–*

74 *Prince Emich of Leiningen 1926–* = Duchess Eilika of Oldenberg

80 *Prince Karl of Leiningen 1928–* = Princess Marie-Louise of Bulgaria

Princess Margarita 1932 (dis.)*

85 *Princess Mechtilde 1936–* = Karl Bauscher

83 *Prince Friedrich of Leiningen 1938–*

69 *Dimitrye K. George 1965–*

81 *Prince Karl 1960–*

82 *Prince Hermann 1963–*

86 *Ulf Bauscher 1963–*

87 *Berthold Bauscher 1965–*

88 *Johan Bauscher 1971–*

75 *Prince Karl 1952–* = Princess Margarite of Hohenloche-Ochringen

76 *Prince Andreas 1955–* = Princess Alexandra of Hanover

79 *Princess Stephanie 1958–*

77 *Prince Ferdinand 1982–*

* (dis.) = *disqualified by marriage to a Roman Catholic*

↓ = *issue not relevant*

CONTENTS

INTRODUCTION

The portly and dissolute King Farouk of Egypt predicted, at about the middle of the present century, that by the year 2000 there would be only five monarchs left in Europe: the four kings in a pack of cards, and the King of England.

With less than 15 years to go, his prediction seems unlikely to be fulfilled. for although in the intervening years Greece has lost a monarchy, Spain has regained one. But Farouk was speaking at a time when, after two world wars which reshaped the continent, the resorts of Europe were littered with deposed monarchs – all of them living proof that no king reigns by divine right.

At the beginning of the twentieth century almost every country in Europe, with the notable exceptions of France and Switzerland, had as its head of state a hereditary monarch. Now, a handful of tiny principalities apart, only Great Britain, Norway, Sweden, Denmark, the Netherlands, Belgium and Spain remain as constitutional monarchies.

It was a feature of monarchist Europe that virtually all its royal families were interrelated; monarchy believed that it should not, indeed could not, marry beneath its station. The only suitable marriage partners for princes and princesses were the sons and daughters of other kings and queens. There were not enough children of reigning monarchs to go round to offer a reasonable choice, but there was a huge reservoir of princely blood among those families who had once ruled over

Matriarch of several dynasties: Victoria poses with Albert and 39 of her children, grandchildren, nephews and nieces, c. 1872.

minor north European states until their thrones had been subsumed into the unified nation of Germany.

Thus, in the following pages, as we trace the first 100 people who, on the principle of strict heredity, are in line of succession to the throne of Great Britain, we find that the trail meanders through a good many of the royal houses of Europe, both reigning and deposed.

The common factor, and fount of the entire 100, is Queen Victoria, who herself married a scion of a minor German royal house, Prince Albert of Saxe-Coburg-Gotha. Victoria had nine children, and yet by the time we reach our 100th candidate, the descendants of her first two sons have not been exhausted. At a conservative estimate, there are over 300 direct descendants of Victoria living today.

Of course this entire thesis is a theoretical exercise, for it presupposes that heredity is the only qualification for monarchy. This is patently not so.

Elizabeth II, queen of Great Britain and of sixteen other realms and territories, reigns, according to her full titles, By the Grace of God. But the Almighty really has very little to do with it. Elizabeth can· trace a line of blood descent back through all 62 previous English monarchs to Egbert of Wessex, generally recognized as the first king of the English in AD 827, making the monarchy the oldest secular institution in the United Kingdom.

But in reality Elizabeth II reigns by the grace of 12 and 13 William III, cap 2, 1702, commonly known as the Act of Settlement. Were heredity the only criterion, we in Great Britain should now be reigned over by Albert Duke of Bavaria, a 70-year-old recluse who lives the life of a minor German aristocrat in the lonely splendour of Schloss Nymphenburg outside Munich.

Duke Albert's position as pretender to the British throne arises from his direct descent from the Stuart kings of Britain. That his residence today is Munich and not Buckingham Palace is entirely due to the Act of Settlement, proof beyond measure that monarchs ultimately reign, not by birthright, but by the will of the people.

James II of Great Britain was the last Roman Catholic king of a predominantly Protestant nation. His flight and subsequent defeat by the Protestant William of Orange at the Battle of the Boyne in 1690, an event remembered with undue obsession by the Protestant community of Northern Ireland, persuaded the British Parliament to take steps to ensure that his descendants never again occupied the British throne.

They tried, of course. In 1715 the Old Pretender and 30 years later the Young Pretender, Prince Charles Edward Stuart, attempted to recapture the throne for the Stuarts, but both were soundly defeated by force of arms and public apathy, at least outside the Scottish Highlands which to this day retain pockets of fervent Catholicism.

James II's second daughter Queen Anne did in fact occupy the throne, but she was tolerated because of her Protestant upbringing. The 1702 Act of Settlement ensured that she would be the last of the Stuarts.

The Act declared that in the event of Anne leaving no lawful heirs, the British crown should pass to the Electress Sophia of Hanover, a descendant of James I of England and VI of Scotland through his daughter Elizabeth of Bohemia (the so-called 'Winter Queen'). Had this book been compiled in 1702, Sophia of Hanover would have figured close to the bottom of the list, or possibly off it altogether; her relationship to the joint reigning monarchs William III and Mary II, and to their successor Queen Anne, was remote, but everyone in line of succession above her was either a Roman Catholic or married to one. She was therefore the first available Protestant.

In the event, Sophia died shortly before Queen Anne, and the British crown passed to Sophia's son the Elector of Hanover, who arrived in London,

Before the Revolution: Tsar Nicholas II of Russia and some of his royal relations. (L to r): Queen Alexandra of Great Britain, Princess Ingeborg of Denmark, the Duchess of Oldenburg (the Tsar's sister), the Tsaritsa, Princess Victoria, the Tsar, King Edward VII of Great Britain, Queen Maud of Norway, Prince Harald of Denmark, King Haakon of Norway, the Queen of Denmark and the King of Denmark, with the Tsar's three elder daughters.

speaking no English, to rule as George I. From him all succeeding British monarchs are descended in a relatively direct line.

The Act of Settlement remains on the statute books, and even today, in a supposedly ecumenical age, it occasionally surfaces to wag an admonitory finger at British royalty's dealings with Roman Catholicism. Anyone who professes the Catholic faith or marries a Catholic is still automatically debarred from the British line of succession.

Apart from religion, the only other ground for disqualification from the British line of succession is birth out of wedlock. There are several examples in that category who are mentioned in the body of the book.

Otherwise, the Royal 100 earn their places strictly on the grounds of heredity. It is a significant change from the beginning of the century that a number of them are commoners, although the majority remain offspring of regal or princely families. Many of the foreigners have, for various reasons, close connections with Britain, and some of them live here. Theoretically they are all British subjects, as the Act of Settlement naturalized the Electress Sophia of Hanover and her complete issue. Many struggle to keep alight the flame of their own deposed monarchies. But few below the obvious candidates at the top of the list harbour the slightest belief or desire that they will ever sit in Westminster Abbey to have the Crown of St Edward placed upon their head.

The Windsor dynasty which currently occupies the British throne, patently with the overwhelming consent of the British people, seems assured of a long tenure – always provided of course that the political climate of the nation continues to find a hereditary monarchy a desirable institution. The Prince of Wales, heir to the throne, has two children of his own, will probably have more, and has two brothers and a sister. So it will have to be a disaster or political upheaval of spectacular proportions before a government has to go beyond Queen Elizabeth II's own children and grandchildren to find an occupant for the British throne. If it is to be revolution or invasion, then it must be assumed that the institution will be swept away altogether, and books like this will become not only even more of a historical curiosity, but also will probably be banned.

To guide the reader along the winding trail of heredity which follows, a brief outline of the rules may be helpful.

The principles of succession to the British throne are simple enough, apart from the disqualifications of Catholicism and illegitimacy mentioned above. The departed sovereign is succeeded by his or her sons in descending order of age. Therefore Prince Charles, the eldest son, will succeed his mother Elizabeth II. The eldest son of Edward VII, Albert Duke of Clarence, predeceased his father, and the crown therefore passed to Edward's second son, who reigned as George V.

If there are no sons, the departed sovereign is succeeded by his or her daughters in descending order of age. Thus George VI was succeeded by his elder daughter Elizabeth II.

If the departed sovereign has no children, he or she is succeeded by any brothers in descending order of age. Thus was the childless Edward VIII succeeded on his abdication by the eldest of his brothers, George VI. Had George previously died or, as he very nearly did, refused the crown, it would have passed to Edward's next brother Henry Duke of Gloucester, and the monarch today would be Henry's son the present Duke, reigning as King Richard IV.

If the departed sovereign's brothers have all predeceased him or her, the search goes through each of them in descending order of age to discover if they have left any children. If the first brother left sons, they will succeed in descending order of age; if there are no sons, then his daughters will succeed in order of age. This was the route by which the longest-reigning of all British monarchs attained the throne. William IV succeeded his brother George IV, who had died without legitimate heirs. William in his turn had several sons, but they were all illegitimate. His two legitimate daughters both died young, before their father had even ascended the throne, so he left no issue to succeed him. The search moved to his next brother in order of age, Edward Duke of Kent. Edward had no sons but he had a daughter – her name was Victoria.

If the departed sovereign's first brother had died leaving no children, the search would move to the

Before the abdication: Elizabeth with her uncle King Edward VIII.

next dead brother to see if he had any children. Only when all the brothers and their lack of children had been exhausted would the same search be conducted through the dead sovereign's sisters, in descending order of age, and their children. So Mary I succeeded her childless brother Edward VI in 1553; Mary was succeeded in turn by her sister Elizabeth I in 1558.

The departed sovereign's spouse plays no part in the succession. Except in the unique case of William and Mary, who ruled jointly, the monarch reigns alone. The spouse's role in perpetuating the dynasty ends with the act of procreation.

The practice of male heirs taking precedence at every stage of the succession, even over elder sisters, is firmly rooted in the principle of primogeniture – eldest son takes all – which for centuries has been the English aristocracy's guiding light in the handing down of property. Its benefit has been that many of the great estates have remained intact instead of being subdivided over and over again among all the children of the deceased.

But there are even more sexist systems. The Roman Catholic monarchies of Spain and Belgium operate under Salic law, which dictates that a woman cannot succeed to the throne at all – when a sovereign dies the search must begin for the nearest male heir, however distantly related he might be. The Protestant throne of Norway operates the same principle; but although the daughter of a Norwegian king cannot become Queen of Norway, she could in theory become Queen of England.

The Swedes, as might be expected of such a race of social pioneers, have done away not only with Salic law but with primogeniture; since 1979 the right of succession to the Swedish throne has passed to the sovereign's eldest child irrespective of sex. Europe's three other non-Salic thrones, those of Britain, the Netherlands and Denmark, are all currently occupied by women.

Although the order of succession is in general rigidly adhered to, several monarchs have ascended the English throne by highly tortuous routes, usually for reasons of political pressure or force of arms. Almost always, however, some blood tie, distant though it might be, has been claimed.

The Saxon kings followed broadly the hereditary principle but did not apply it at all rigidly. Indeed the Witan, an assembly of earls, magnates and clergy which was pre-Norman England's closest approximation to Parliament, had an elective role in the choice of monarch; it chose Harold for his experience and maturity to succeed Edward the Confessor in preference to the true heir Edgar Atheling who was deemed too young to rule the unruly land. Harold's sister had been the Confessor's wife but, under the rules of succession, that was a somewhat irrelevant consideration.

William of Normandy's claim to the English throne rested chiefly on his assertion that he had been promised it by the Confessor, although there was also a tenuous blood connection: the Confessor's mother was the sister of William's grandfather. But as William was a bastard son he had no real claim at all.

Henry Tudor, an obscure Welsh prince, took the throne by force of arms, ending the fifteenth-century rivalry for the crown between the dynasties of Lancaster and York. But he still had a claim of sorts to the succession: his grandfather Owen Tudor had married Catherine, widow of Henry V.

Elizabeth I died childless, having outlived all her brothers, sisters and cousins. The crown passed to James VI of Scotland, partly because there was a political will at the time for a union of the two kingdoms, and partly because his great-grandmother Margaret Tudor, wife of James IV of Scotland and sister of Henry VIII, had been Elizabeth I's aunt. With two kingdoms under his belt, King James, 'the wisest fool in Christendom',

Above: the Queen and Prince Philip on their way to the coronation, in June 1953.

Right: Prince Charles and Princess Anne study a world of shrinking red.

postulated the theory that kings reigned by Divine Right; the theory collapsed when his son Charles I lost his head at the hands of Cromwell's Parliamentarians.

Monarchy is mystique. One of the reasons it survives so well in Britain seems to be because there is no written constitution to delineate its powers. To define its role is to diminish its influence, as has happened to the 'bicycling monarchies' of north-western continental Europe. The power of the British monarch is not so much illusory as elusive. Certainly its rights are severely circumscribed, as over seven centuries Parliament and people have nibbled away at its direct powers, chiefly as a protection against bad monarchs, of which we have had our fair share.

Yet within its constitutional limits, the influence of the monarchy remains great and its very existence remains a powerful totem for the unity and continuity of the nation. Some of the people who figure in this book are the descendants of indifferent monarchs who contributed to the demise of their own thrones; many had their thrones swept away on tides of revolution and war. But the Windsor dynasty has been particularly adept at giving the British people the kind of monarchy they want.

*Although the Royal 100 was a correct list at the time of going to press, it must be remembered that births and deaths create a constantly changing picture.

THE
ROYAL HOUSE
OF
Windsor

*A galaxy of European monarchy assembled at Buckingham Palace
for the wedding of Prince Charles and Lady Diana Spencer.
Children in the front row (l to r): Edward van Cutsam, the Earl of
Ulster, Catherine Cameron, Clementine Hambro, Sarah Jane
Gaselee, Lord Nicholas Windsor. Second row (l to r): King Carl
Gustav and Queen Silvia of Sweden; King Baudouin and Queen
Fabiola of the Belgians; Princess Margaret; Princess Anne; the
Queen Mother; the Queen; India Hicks; Lady Sarah Armstrong-
Jones; Hon. Mrs Frances Shand-Kydd; Earl Spencer; Lady Sarah
McCorquodale; Neil McCorquodale; Queen Beatrix of the
Netherlands; Lady Helen Windsor; Grand Duke Jean and Grand
Duchess Josephine Charlotte of Luxembourg. Third row (l to r): the
Prince of Denmark; Queen Margrethe of Denmark; King Olav of
Norway; James and Marina Ogilvy; Captain Mark Phillips; Hon.
Angus Ogilvy; Princess Alexandra; Prince Andrew; Viscount Linley;
the Duchess of Gloucester; Prince Philip; the Duke of Gloucester;
Prince Edward; Princess Alice, Duchess of Gloucester; the Prince of
Wales; the Duke of Kent (behind Ruth, Lady Fermoy); the Earl of St
Andrews (behind the Prince of Wales); the Duchess of Kent; Lady
Jane Fellowes; behind her, Viscount Althorp; Robert Fellowes;
Prince and Princess Michael of Kent; Princess Grace of Monaco;
Prince Albert of Monaco; immediately below him, Prince Claus of the
Netherlands; Princess Gina and Prince Franz Josef of Liechtenstein.*

1

Prince Charles is invested at Caernarfon Castle, 1969.

Charles Philip Arthur George, known as HRH to his staff, Wales to his friends, and Taffy Windsor to his former shipmates in the Royal Navy, was born to an awesome destiny from which he cannot readily escape.

He was born on 14 November 1948 at Buckingham Palace, the first child of the Duke of Edinburgh and the then Princess Elizabeth. He was born a prince of the royal blood, but strictly speaking no more than that; his mother was heiress presumptive, the presumption being that she would inherit the throne only if her father George VI produced no sons to take automatic precedence over her. Such an event was of course most unlikely; the King was already aged 52, in failing health, and had fathered his last child, Princess Margaret, 18 years before.

When the King died in 1952 leaving only daughters, the elder ascended the throne as Queen Elizabeth II, and her eldest son automatically became heir apparent; from that moment no one could take precedence over Charles, and only his own refusal, abdication,

incapacity or death could open the throne to anyone else.

If Charles ascends the throne he will follow Victoria, Edward VII, George V, George VI and Elizabeth II as the sixth generation of a direct line of descent from parent to child, a straight run unmatched in the often wayward history of the British Crown since the days of the early Plantagenet kings.

He boasts a pedigree that is frightening in its extent. In 1977, at the age of 92, Mr Gerald Paget of Welwyn Garden City, Hertfordshire, produced his first and only book, in two volumes costing £60,

The future C III R? Prince Charles, patron of the Royal Opera, on stage at Covent Garden.

and entitled *The Lineage and Ancestry of HRH Prince Charles, Prince of Wales*. Mr Paget, an amateur genealogist of astonishing patience, traced and enumerated 262,142 ancestors of Prince Charles. It was a slight cheat, for as a result of cousin marriages many of that number are in fact the same person appearing several times; inbreeding has always been a strong strand in royal pedigrees. Nevertheless Mr Paget showed that

Prince Charles was in some way descended from just about everybody who was anybody, anywhere, ever.

Among his more direct forbears are the royal houses of Scotland, France, Germany, Austria, Denmark, Sweden, Norway, Spain, Portugal, Russia and the Netherlands. He can trace a connection to Alfred the Great, Hereward the Wake, William the Conqueror and every English monarch since (but not, apparently, to Oliver Cromwell). He is descended no fewer than 22 times over from Mary Queen of Scots, and at least once from the Welsh prince Owen Glendower, the Irish high king Brian Boru, Robert the Bruce of Scotland, Sven Forkbeard the Viking, Catherine the Great of Russia, Good King Wenceslas of Bohemia, the emperors Charlemagne and Frederick Barbarossa, Frederick the Great of Prussia, Pope Nicholas II, and last but far from least among mere commoners, George Washington.

'Prince of Wales' has been the title given to the monarch's eldest son ever since Edward I, having routed the last of the native Welsh princes Llewelyn ap Gruffydd ap Llewelyn in 1282, held up his infant son, the future Edward II, from the ramparts of his new Caernarfon Castle and presented him to the Welsh people. The young Edward was not invested with his new title formally until some years later and that event, it must be said, took place far from Wales, at Lincoln.

Charles is the twenty-first Prince of Wales, yet strangely only 13 of the previous holders of the title ever became king, and one of those was Edward VIII, who did not stay at his post long enough for his Coronation. The previous line of Welsh princes stretches back from Llewelyn to Rhodri the Great in the ninth century, when the fierce Welsh tribes of ancient British stock had little truck with the Saxon English.

Princess Elizabeth, in 1948, was only the fourth heiress presumptive in British history to give birth to a male child, and so far only one of those

Mr Fixit: Prince Charles with his great-uncle, Earl Mountbatten.

children has become king, as Henry II. Charles was the first child born in direct line of succession to the British throne since Edward VIII, eldest son of George V, 54 years earlier.

The odds on a prince of Wales becoming king are therefore not quite as certain as might be imagined, even in recent times. But assuming Charles stays the course, how will he style himself? He himself has said that he will reign as King Charles III, although he would be quite entitled to call himself King Philip, King Arthur II, King George VII, or indeed any other name he cared to choose. Philip is a mite too Spanish, Arthur historically shaky, George frankly dull; Charles III restores some respectability to the Stuart kings who bore the name in the seventeenth century.

Christening the child Charles was in itself a nod to the Stuarts by his mother, for the name had virtually disappeared from British royal usage since the arrival of the Hanoverians, to whom it smacked too much of Jacobitism. Philip is the name of his father, and Arthur and George are two names favoured by Victoria and a great many of her descendants.

There is the question of Prince Charles' surname, which is not quite so well defined. On the principle that children take the surname of their father – even royal princes who rarely, if ever, use a surname – he should be Charles Mountbatten. Mountbatten was the name adopted by the Duke of Edinburgh, born without obvious surname as plain Prince Philip of Greece. It was the surname of his English uncle Louis Mountbatten; Mountbatten's father was actually called Battenberg but the name was anglicized in 1914 when he, a German, found himself First Lord of the Admiralty at war with his native land. To be historically pedantic, the Prince of Wales should be called Charles Philip Arthur George Schleswig-Holstein-Sonderburg-Glucksburg, since if Philip of Greece had a surname at all, that was what it would have been, considering his descent from the Greek and Danish royal houses.

Queen Elizabeth put paid to the remotest possibility of any such nonsense when she ascended the throne in 1952, declaring in an Order in Council that she and her descendants would be known as the family and house of Windsor. From being Charles Mountbatten (although no one ever called him that) the heir apparent became, and remains, Charles Windsor. In 1960 the Queen rather confused the issue by appearing to change her mind, decreeing in a further Order that any of her descendants not graced with the title of Prince or Princess should bear the surname Mountbatten-Windsor, in recognition of her husband's contribution to the dynasty. Although it was not strictly necessary for her to do so, Princess Anne signed herself Anne Mountbatten-Windsor in her marriage register.

The present heir to the throne has been a pioneer, both witting and unwitting, in a number of respects. He was the first heir to the throne to be born without the presence of the Home Secretary of the day at the confinement bedside, a practice that appears to have dated from 1688 when Mary of Modena, wife of James II, was suspected of substituting a changeling for the heir to the throne, in an episode known as the Incident of the Warming-pan. George VI thought the practice outmoded and ridiculous, and sensibly dispensed with it. As Duke of York, he had had to go along with this custom when his own children were born; the Home Secretary of the day, William Joynson-Hicks, had waited with great unease in the corner of a bedroom at 17 Bruton Street, London on 21 April 1926, while the future Queen Elizabeth II was delivered by Caesarean section. Her own heir would be delivered without this additional presence; Prince Charles' facial features are an assurance that he is no one other than who he claims to be.

Prince Charles was also the first heir to the throne to go to school, a decision taken with some trepidation by his parents as it placed him at serious risk of exposure to journalists. While he was at Hill House pre-preparatory school in Knightsbridge, his mother threatened to take him away unless the photographers left him alone. Their consciences at least temporarily pricked, the hounds withdrew. He then went to Cheam in Berkshire, one-time *alma mater* of that academic dunce Winston Churchill, and then to Gordonstoun, a tough Scottish public school 600 miles from London and its newspaper offices. His brisk and impatient father had relished the physical rigours of Gordonstoun, but the more sensitive Charles did not.

Charles was not the first heir to the throne to attend university, but he was certainly the first to attend a full degree course, and to graduate. Scraping into Trinity College, Cambridge, on school examination qualifications that the Cambridge entrance board might have regarded in lesser mortals as exceedingly borderline, Charles in fact proved a dedicated and able undergraduate. For the first part of his three-year course he chose to study anthropology and archaeology, a recognized option of arts undergraduates with no leaning to any obvious specialization, switching to his real love of history for his second part. He graduated from Cambridge with a lower second-class degree. The Master of Trinity, Lord Butler of Saffron Walden, offered the view that had he stuck with his original subjects and had he not been constantly interrupted by the pressures of royal business, especially his investiture as Prince of Wales at Caernarfon in 1969, he would have won a first comfortably.

Prince Charles' subsequent career in the Royal Navy was one of the happier episodes of his life, if only because a ship at sea affords an unrivalled measure of privacy from cameras and curious eyes. He eventually graduated to command one of the oldest and smallest ships in the Navy, the wooden-hulled minesweeper *HMS Bronington*. Retirement from seafaring at the tender age of 29

happily coincided with his mother's Silver Jubilee in 1977. There was some immediate and obvious work for him to do in administering the Jubilee charitable trusts, while at the same time looking after his 130,000 acres of inherited property, the Duchy of Cornwall.

With little to do but rehearse endlessly for his eventual role, the Prince soon began to exhibit to his close friends signs of frustration and boredom, and it was no surprise when he took himself a wife in 1981. Since then he has become deeply immersed in the pleasures of family life and young children, which have restored to him some immediate and obvious sense of purpose.

He has, of course, been groomed for kingship from an early age. His mother, carefully avoiding the error of Queen Victoria who would not let her eldest son, the future Edward VII, see her State papers, has shared with Charles the confidences of monarchy so that he may know what to expect from his twice-daily boxes of government papers that must be read. He has been made acquainted with every conceivable facet of British life, from meetings of the Privy Council to the annual conference of a trade union (admittedly a safely right-wing one, the Iron and Steel Trades Confederation). He shoulders more than his share of overseas official visits, a duty that is bound to increase as the Queen grows older and her energy declines. He is immensely popular and well-liked, not least because he has the saving graces of occasional self-deprecation and a slightly askew sense of humour.

Prince Charles has had a broader education, in every respect, than any of his predecessors, and enjoys a less formal relationship with his subjects than any previous heir to the throne could have contemplated. He is rich; the Duchy of Cornwall is now yielding net annual revenues of over £1 million and since his marriage Charles has taken three-quarters for himself, donating the balance to the State purses in lieu of the income tax from which, happy man, he is exempt.

He wants for little, except perhaps privacy and a more clearly defined job than he has at present. The job will come in time, and he will have been uniquely and exhaustively trained for it. And yet, and yet. Are not the great forged on the anvil of oppression? There is no knowing what pressures the throne will be under by the time he ascends it, and the century is likely to have turned before that event takes place. Monarchs have little scope for entering truly controversial arenas, although Charles has spoken out boldly on modern architecture, displaying an attitude that is essentially conservative, but at the same time commonsense. He is, in the old terminology, a bit of a square, but perhaps none the worse for that; the people look for stability, but not dullness, in their monarchs.

Charles III is unlikely to be a great pioneer of constitutional monarchy, but then neither have any of his immediate forbears shown a taste for sudden change or innovation. The house of Windsor has had two particular talents: for steering well clear of political controversy, unlike Victoria who occasionally thought she knew better than Gladstone, and told him so; and for recognizing what kind of monarchy the people want, and adjusting to it by slow evolution. Informality is the key of the age, although the pendulum could perfectly easily swing back to a desire for remote grandeur.

The new King must pray for a continuation of the fair wind that has blown the British monarchy along with its people for so long, and he will doubtless guard against any incipient tendency for the royal family to become merely another soap opera. Barring revolution, Charles III will be the head of State of the largest constitutional monarchy remaining in the world, the incumbent of the highest remaining office on earth attained by birthright. The first duty of all British monarchs is to ensure that they are not the last.

The Princess of Wales walked down the aisle followed by 25 feet of ivory silk.

Stealing the show: Prince William is the centre of attention after the christening of his younger brother Prince Henry.

2

Prince William of Wales

William Arthur Philip Louis Windsor, Prince William of Wales, or plain 'Wills' to his father, is, by the calculation of the genealogists, destined to be the most British of British monarchs since James I.

James I, the son of Mary, Queen of Scots and her second husband Henry Darnley, was also James VI of Scotland, and was deemed to be 75 per cent Scots. If Englishness is the required standard of purity, we must go back to Elizabeth I, who by descent was almost pure English. According to the mathematicians of *Burke's Peerage*, Prince William is 39 per cent English, 16 per cent Scots, 6.25 per cent Irish, 6.25 per cent American, the balance being made up from dashes of Greek, Danish, German, Russian and Polish, chiefly from his paternal grandfather Prince Philip, Duke of Edinburgh, whose family tree winds through most of the royal houses of Europe both existing and defunct.

Young William has at least 27 separate lines of descent from Mary, Queen of Scots, 22 through his father and at least five through his mother. When he eventually succeeds to the throne, which in theory should be about the year 2030 if the present Queen and her successor Charles III both enjoy a full and healthy span, William V will be the forty-second monarch since William the Conqueror, the seventh generation of a direct line of descent from Victoria, and the twelfth in direct descent from the Electress Sophia of Hanover. At the root of William's claim to the throne is the 1702 Act of Settlement which gave the British crown to Sophia and her descendants on the death of Queen Anne.

William was the first child born to a Prince of Wales since 1905. He will become heir apparent to the throne on the accession of his father as Charles III. He cannot be preceded in his claim by any

children born after him. He will be the first King William since William IV (1830–37) and will pray that he is not known, like his ancestor, as Silly Billy.

William brings into the royal line the fresh blood of the Spencer family through his mother Diana, Princess of Wales, daughter of the 8th Earl Spencer. The Spencers grew to be one of England's richest families on the back of the country's once-massive wool trade, but none of them had ever before married into royalty. Yet the Spencer blood is not quite as fresh a strand as it might seem.

Prince Charles and Princess Diana are in fact seventh cousins, and have a common ancestor in William Cavendish, 3rd Duke of Devonshire (1698–1755). His son the 4th Duke was the great-great-grandfather of Nina Cavendish-Bentinck, mother of Queen Elizabeth the Queen Mother, who is William's great-grandmother. Meanwhile, the 3rd Duke of Devonshire's daughter Elizabeth Cavendish had a direct descendant who married the 6th Earl Spencer, great-grandfather of Princess Diana. Elizabeth Cavendish is therefore Diana's six-times-great grandmother.

Diana also descends from a Spencer line that was the result of a liaison between Charles II and one of his mistresses. Wrong side of the blanket it may have been, but Diana has brought a little of the blood of the Stuart kings back into the royal line.

Prince William was born on 21 June 1982, the year of the Falklands War and the first visit to Britain by a reigning pope. His birthplace was most unkingly; until Princess Anne set a new fashion, all royal babies had entered the world in the grand surroundings of their royal homes. But not for William; he first saw the light inside the drab and unromantic Lindo Wing of St Mary's Hospital in Paddington, a down-at-heel and workaday corner of London that overlooks the railway yards. Future generations who seek out the plaque that will one day be erected to mark the birthplace of a king are likely to be in for a considerable disappointment.

Since Princess Anne had her two children there, all royal births have been conducted in St Mary's, at the gentle but firm insistence of Mr George Pinker, the Queen's gynaecologist, whose view of childbirth is that nothing should be left to chance, and that a well-equipped hospital is the best place to be in case there are unexpected difficulties or complications. The choice of St Mary's is simply because that happens to be Mr Pinker's hospital.

The Princess of Wales took a private room at £140 a night, into which was installed special equipment should she decide to opt for the position, currently fashionable in France, of giving birth standing up. She did not. Not only was it the first hospital birth for an heir to the throne, it was the first at which the father was present throughout. While Prince Charles was being born at Buckingham Palace, his father the Duke of Edinburgh played squash with one of his staff. And while each of his six children was being born, George V sat stoically in another room reading *Pilgrim's Progress*. Prince Charles clearly relished the experience, and was present again for the birth of Prince Harry.

Prince William's upbringing, in tune with the age, has also been somewhat unconventional for one born to such high station. Not for him an early childhood with nannies and governesses, only to be shown to his parents, scrubbed and powdered, just before bedtime. He has had far more contact with his parents than anyone previously born to his position, and enjoys something approaching a normal family life.

He has a nanny, the informal Miss Barbara Barnes, who refuses to wear a uniform, but his mother plays a major part in his upbringing, and he is probably the first heir to the throne to have had his nappies changed by his father. His parents will probably stop short of educating him at a State school, if only because of the problems of privacy and security such a choice would pose, but in most other respects he can look forward to an upbringing which, although hardly average, will be a great deal less rarified, stiff and formal than that suffered by his predecessors.

It will all lead, in the long run, to a certain demystification of the office of monarchy, and a moderation of its deification. By the time he ascends the throne, William will feel, and will be perceived as, less different from the rest of us than previous sovereigns. Whether that is a good thing for the institution is arguable; monarchy is a magnificent show that relies heavily on mystique, and its supporters would regard it as a great shame if the British monarchy, the most magnificent still in existence, were reduced to the humble level of the 'bicycling monarchies' of north-west Europe.

Above: brotherly love: Prince William, aged 2¼, holds his brother Prince Harry, aged 3 weeks.

Opposite: fast learner: Prince William, aged 2, displays an early mastery of the royal wave.

It is some time since a monarch cried: 'God for Harry, England and St George'. The first name of Prince Henry Charles Albert David, second son of the Prince of Wales, is not without controversy.

Prince Harry, as he is universally and more or less officially known, breaks with recent tradition; no other member of the royal family currently bears the name. The last was Prince Henry, third son of George V who became Duke of Gloucester, and the last monarch to bear it was Henry VIII, best known for his six wives. Should Harry ever ascend the throne – and there is no shortage of precedents for the second-born doing so – he would be entitled to call himself Henry IX, although there is no law nor unshakable convention that compels the monarch to rule under his first baptismal name. As Henry IX he would be the first Ninth of any name.

Those Jacobites who still drink to 'the King over

the water' will also be aware that somewhere among the descendants of the last Stuart king, James II, a Roman Catholic who fled a predominantly Protestant nation, there was a man who claimed to be King Henry IX of Great Britain. But after the failed efforts of the Old Pretender, James Stuart, in 1715, and the Young Pretender, Bonnie Prince Charlie, in 1745, the Jacobite cause is now a part of distant history, and that Henry IX is long dead.

Had Bonnie Prince Charlie succeeded in his campaign, he would have reigned as Charles III, thus depriving the present Prince of Wales of his proposed title. But then, of course, the present Prince of Wales would be somebody entirely different, and Prince Harry, if he existed at all, would be plain Mr Harry Windsor, a jolly fellow who would command attention at parties by telling everyone how, had the Hanoverians been allowed to continue reigning in Britain, he would be in line for the British throne.

The choice of both William and Harry as first names is evidence of Princess Diana's influence at work. Asked about the choice of William, Prince Charles merely smiled diplomatically and explained that it was chosen because neither parent had any close relative of that name. For the choice of Harry, he had no explanation at all.

Prince Harry's second name of Charles comes most obviously from his father, but also from his maternal uncle, Viscount Althorp, Diana's brother and the heir to the Spencer earldom. As for Albert, it has long been popular in the house of Windsor as a memorial to Victoria's greatly beloved consort. From the old German, meaning 'noble and bright', it was the name of Diana's grandfather, and the first name of George VI, who was known to his family as Bertie but who chose to reign under one of his middle names in an effort to give some continuity after the trauma of Edward VIII's abdication. (Edward VIII was actually christened, and known to his parents as, David).

The inclusion of David in the child's names is not so much a recognition of the abdicated King as a nod in the direction of Queen Elizabeth the Queen Mother, whose favourite brother out of a very large family was David Bowes-Lyon.

Harry, like his brother, was born in St Mary's Hospital, Paddington, on 15 September 1984, when his mother was a tender 23 years old. It was an uncomplicated birth and, in common with contemporary practice, mother and child were despatched home less than 24 hours after the event, to the waiting nursery at Kensington Palace, where his parents enjoy rent-free and spacious accommodation by courtesy of the Queen.

Harry immediately assumed third place in line of succession after Prince Charles and Prince William. It is worth remembering that in the history of the house of Windsor, fate has cast the second-born on to the throne with remarkable frequency. Edward VII, Queen Victoria's second child, succeeded because her first-born was a daughter. George V succeeded because his elder brother the Duke of Clarence died prematurely. George VI succeeded because his elder brother chose Mrs Wallis Warfield Simpson in preference to his inherited duty.

There is little to record of one so young, except that he does not fly in the same aircraft as his slightly older brother. Great was the consternation when Prince Charles took his first-born with him in an Andover of the Queen's Flight to Aberdeen en route to Balmoral; it was a journey undertaken only after close consultation with the Queen, a discussion coloured by the insistence of William's parents that royal protocol and precedent were not going to come between a father and his son more than was absolutely necessary. Charles and Diana took William with them to Australia, but had to leave him behind for his first birthday when they went to Canada. Harry, the royal backstop, is fated forever to fly in a separate aircraft from his big brother.

4

Prince Andrew

Prince Andrew, second son and third child of the Queen, was born second in line to the throne after his elder brother Prince Charles, but as all present and future children of Prince Charles take precedence over him, his position has already declined to the point where there is no longer any great likelihood of his being a serious contender for the throne.

Since his twenty-first birthday he has been a Counsellor of State, empowered to act on behalf of the Queen when she is out of the country. His only other potential constitutional role would be that of Regent; such a possibility would require that

Once dubbed Randy Andy, Prince Andrew has gained a reputation from the dailies as heartthrob and hero.

Queen Elizabeth and her husband were both dead, and that King Charles III had also died prematurely, at an age when his successor Prince William was still too young to reign. The situation cannot be regarded as likely.

Andrew Albert Christian Edward, named firstly after his paternal grandfather Prince Andrew of Greece, was born at Buckingham Palace on 19 February 1960, ten years after his sister Princess Anne. The gap was caused by the Queen's accession in 1952. A combination of inexperience and dedication persuaded Elizabeth to give her undivided attention to her constitutional position for seven years before she felt sufficiently confident to take time off for a further bout of motherhood.

After early education by governesses and at Heatherdown preparatory school near Ascot, Prince Andrew followed his father and elder brother to Gordonstoun, where he enjoyed the robust way of life, with its emphasis on physical fitness, rather more than the sensitive Prince Charles. Andrew managed to collect four 'A' level passes, travelled to France and Germany to improve his languages, and spent two terms at Lakefield College School, Ontario. His subsequent career has been a conventional one for a sovereign's son: after graduating from the Royal Naval College at Dartmouth he took on a 12-year commission at sea.

Prince Andrew's career as a naval helicopter pilot, which included a spell of front-line active service in the Falklands War of 1982, has greatly enhanced his manly and daredevil reputation, although his mother has occasionally felt obliged to warn him against a certain tendency towards arrogance. Andrew has caused the Queen his fair share of worry, over his safety at war and his subsequent quest for light relief among young women whose pedigree has not always been quite what the royal family would have chosen.

When Prince Andrew turned 18 in 1978 he became eligible for an allowance of £20,000 a year from the Civil List, but the Queen decided that he should receive only £8,000 of it, to offset the cost of a secretary to deal with his mail both official and adulatory. The balance was invested by the Royal Trustees for his future use. But since his twenty-first birthday, an event marked by a dinner party and ball at Windsor Castle, he has drawn the full amount. As with all Civil List payments, this income is intended only to cover the expenses of his currently minimal official duties, and not for pocket money. He is liable for income tax on any part of it not used strictly for official purposes.

Prince Andrew, being so close to the throne, may look forward to a heavy burden of official duties, although at present his full-time naval career severely limits his public appearances. By far his best-known role to date was to act as joint best man, or supporter, at his brother's wedding to Lady Diana Spencer in St Paul's Cathedral in 1981. Later that year he made his first official public appearance at the Varsity rugby match at Twickenham, and made his first public speech at the subsequent dinner at the Hilton Hotel.

Andrew has conducted two major solo overseas engagements, both with a naval connection. He went to the remote island of St Helena in 1984 to mark 150 years of British colonization; and back to the Falklands in 1985 to declare open the new airport that brought the remote South Atlantic islands within reach of civilization and the Jumbo Jet for the first time.

Precedent suggests that Andrew will be created Duke of York, a title traditionally bestowed on the sovereign's second son.

5

Prince Edward

The third son of a monarch has not succeeded to the throne since 1830, when William IV, third son of George III, succeeded on the death of his eldest brother George IV, who left no living children. Their middle brother, Frederick Duke of York, had predeceased them both.

Prince Edward, third son of the Queen, was born third in line; he has been demoted to fifth by the birth of Prince Charles' two children, and will be further demoted by any more additions to that family, and also by any family which Prince Andrew may sire.

Born at Buckingham Palace on 10 March 1964, he was christened Edward after eight previous kings, Antony after Lord Snowdon, Richard after his cousin the Duke of Gloucester, and Louis after two members of Prince Philip's family: his great-grandfather Louis of Hesse and his revered uncle and mentor Louis Mountbatten.

Edward has been widely regarded as the most intellectual of the Queen's four children, but his Gordonstoun school results were only just enough to scrape him a place at Jesus College, Cambridge, to read for a soft-option broad arts degree. In fact, he participated in all of Gordonstoun's allegedly character-building outdoor activities, becoming a proficient skier and qualifying for his private pilot's licence before he left school. As is traditional with Gordonstoun pupils, he spent two terms at a Commonwealth school; for Edward, it was the Collegiate School at Wanganui, New Zealand, where he acted as a house tutor but gave the impression that he was not particularly interested in a teaching career.

Prince Edward's future lies instead with the Royal Marines. Having performed well on a pre-university selection course for potential officers, he is now having his Cambridge education paid for by the service, and as soon as he graduates will proceed to the Marines' training centre at Lympstone in Dorset. He is likely to serve initially as a rifle troop commander in a commando unit.

The Prince is already well travelled. While tutoring in New Zealand he visited the Antarctic, flying to the South Pole to see scientific bases there. On his way back to England he made a short informal tour of the South Pacific. But his official duties are few, and he has been allowed to grow up in as much decent obscurity as any son of the Queen could reasonably expect; some might think that a pity, considering his talent and enthusiasm for acting in Cambridge undergraduate productions.

As he progresses through his academic and military career, Prince Edward will gradually acquire the customary clutch of honorary presidencies and patronages, and he will perform occasional overseas functions as the Queen grows older and becomes less inclined to take on strenuous foreign travel. After a full-time military career he will in all probability follow the example of the present Duke of Kent, who works hard as vice-chairman of the non-political British Overseas Trade Board. Edward may be expected to find a similar post in public life where he can make some genuine contribution to the common weal without stepping into the forbidden arena of party politics.

The Prince may at some stage be created a royal duke, and the long-vacant title of Duke of Sussex has been floated. Such a title on its own would give him no lands, property or wealth; it would merely entitle him to a seat in the House of Lords, assuming the upper chamber of the mother of parliaments has not voted for its own abolition by

Above: Prince Edward shares an informal 18th birthday study in the gardens of Buckingham Palace with his black labrador Frances.

Left: Prince Edward and his team, Jesus College Seconds, in the midst of a 26–3 defeat at the hands of Trinity College.

then. The creation of new hereditary peerages is, however, currently out of fashion. Since Mrs Margaret Thatcher came to power in 1979 she has created only two, both for long and outstanding political service: The Earl of Stockton (Mr Harold Macmillan) and Viscount Whitelaw (Mr William Whitelaw). By a cruel irony, the latter has no sons to inherit the title.

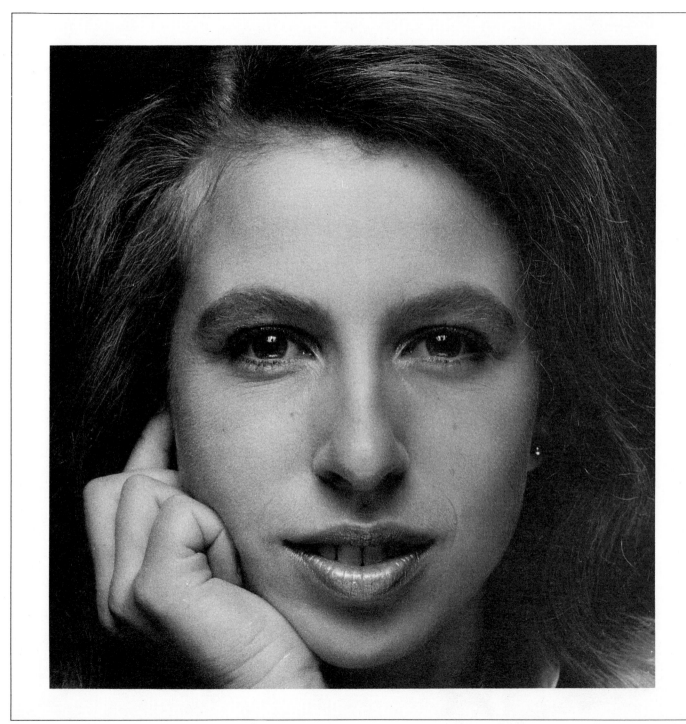

Princess Anne was born third in line to the throne, after her mother, then still Princess Elizabeth, and her brother Charles. For a short period, between Queen Elizabeth's accession and the birth of Prince Andrew, she was second, but she has now descended to sixth, and will slip even further as she is preceded by all future children of her brothers Charles, Andrew and Edward.

Anne Elizabeth Alice Louise was born on 15 August 1950 at Clarence House, the London home of her parents Princess Elizabeth and the Duke of Edinburgh between marriage and accession. She was educated privately at home and in France before becoming a boarder at Benenden in Kent at the age of 12, where she rapidly won herself a place in the school riding team. This was the start of an equestrian career that culminated in a place at the 1976 Olympics in Montreal.

Anne was winning trophies at hunter trials before she left school, but her riding career really

Above: a royal passion for horses is handed down to a young Princess Anne.

Right: with Captain Mark Phillips shortly before their wedding in 1973.

At home: Princess Anne with her baby son, Peter Phillips, in the grounds of Gatcombe Park in 1978.

blossomed when she acquired a horse called Doublet and earned herself a place in the Badminton horse trials. She proceeded to win at the Burghley trials in Lincolnshire, and was a member of the British international team at the European Championships in 1973 and 1975. It was a pity that her crowning achievement in getting to Montreal was dogged by bad luck; she was thrown at one jump and briefly concussed, and the medals went to the United States.

The Princess is an achiever, and it was clear from an early age that, rather than lie back and live off her birthright, attending gala premieres and graciously opening an occasional hospital, she was determined to do something worthwhile in her own right. Her genuine success in the skills of horsemanship was only a beginning.

She has consistently refused any title other than that with which she was born, distancing herself as much as protocol and convention allow from the hothouse of monarchy to create her own life.

The eldest daughter of the sovereign by custom takes the title of Princess Royal, assuming it is vacant (which it is). Anne has rejected all suggestions that she might follow this particular convention, and has equally refused all titles for her husband and children. Her life outside her official duties is that of a gentleman-farmer's wife; she and her husband Captain Mark Phillips, a kindred equestrian spirit, run the 750 acres of Gatcombe Park in Gloucestershire as a commercial farm. Gatcombe was bought for the couple by the Queen as a belated but handsome wedding gift for her daughter, and to give her son-in-law something to do when he left the Army.

At one stage Anne had the reputation, at least among the royalty-watchers of the media, as the rudest and least cooperative member of the entire royal family, with her father nudging below her as a close second. Certainly she has the ability to be haughty, impatient, and intolerant of those who come in her way. She can be the very antithesis of her husband, who appears in public as a man of genial smiles and few words. She is also worlds away from the shy, sugar-sweet image of the Princess of Wales; the two share few common interests, and are unlikely ever to be close friends.

More recently, Princess Anne has been seen in a new and more favourable light. Her frequent overseas visits as president of the Save the Children Fund, usually to the poorest and most desperately down trodden areas of the world, have brought credit to the Princess and no small amount of hard cash to the Fund. She has also achieved much of solid worth as patron of the Riding for the Disabled Association and as president of the British Olympic Association. She is well able to hold her own on television chat shows, although

woe betide any interviewer who oversteps the previously agreed bounds of questioning. She also has the ability on occasion to look exceedingly glamorous, although she is better in full face than in profile; the latter tends to accentuate the rather weak chin and full mouth that are at once recognizable in portraits of George III.

Princess Anne's many other patronages include the British Academy of Film and Television Arts, for which she presents Britain's 'Oscars', London University (of which she is chancellor), the British School of Osteopathy, and the National Union of Townswomen's Guilds, as well as the obligatory portfolio of honorary military appointments.

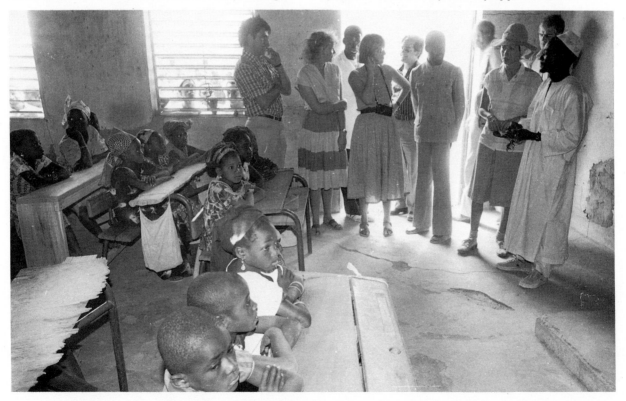

Princess Anne, president of the Save The Children Fund, visits African drought victims at a remote village in Burkina Faso (formerly Upper Volta).

Queen Elizabeth II with her granddaughter, Zara Phillips, in the grounds of Windsor in 1984.

7

Peter Phillips

Peter Phillips is the first grandson of the Queen and the highest commoner in line of succession to the throne. He is the eldest child of Princess Anne, and his lack of title is entirely due to his mother's insistence that it should be so, both for her children and her husband; this did not prevent the Queen from being slightly disappointed that her first grandchild had no ornament to his name beyond plain 'Master'.

Peter Mark Andrew Phillips was born on 15 November 1977, creating another precedent by his very arrival, for he was the first royal baby in living memory not to have been born at home. His mother, not a woman to be intimidated by convention or tradition, chose to have both her children in the Lindo Wing of St Mary's Hospital, Paddington, under the care of Mr George Pinker, the Queen's gynaecologist. She thus set a precedent which her sister-in-law the Princess of Wales was happy to follow when her own children were born.

Peter Phillips is a boisterous, uninhibited child who more than once has had his bottom smacked in public by his mother for misbehaving during horse trials. When very young one of his chosen methods of welcoming visitors to Gatcombe was to enter the drawing room straight from the farmyard and dance on the polished mahogany top of the grand piano in his mud-caked wellingtons.

Peter is already too far removed from the throne to face any great likelihood of a life of public engagements; he is growing up knowing more about the workings of a tractor than the niceties of Court protocol and, naturally, he has had a pony since the age of four. His eventual destiny will be to inherit the estate and farm of Gatcombe Park having first, no doubt, attended a course at the Royal Agricultural College, Cirencester, the premier training school of the English gentleman-farmer. His education began with 24 other four-year-olds at the village nursery school in Minchinhampton, a mile from Gatcombe, and continued at the Blue Boys pre-preparatory school in the same village. On reaching the age of seven in 1984, he was despatched to a preparatory boarding school, Port Regis, near Shaftesbury in Dorset, where efforts continued to instil a measure of decorum into him.

8

Zara Phillips

The second child and first daughter of Princess Anne shares with her father and brother the absence of any title. She too will grow up in the farming tradition established by her paternal grandfather, Major Peter Phillips, who farmed at Tetbury, Gloucestershire, before becoming a director of the Walls meat division of Unilever at Gloucester.

Zara Anne Elizabeth Phillips, born at St Mary's Hospital, Paddington, on 15 May 1981, will spend a considerable part of her life explaining her first name. She will have to repeat many times that she is not named after Zara the Gilbertian princess in *Utopia Limited*, nor is she named after the Italian cruiser *Zara* that her grandfather Prince Philip had a hand in sinking during the Second World War battle of Matapan. Zara, she will reveal, is the Arabic for 'morning star'.

9

Princess Margaret

Zara Phillips ends, for the time being, the direct descendants of Elizabeth II and, unless Princess Anne has another daughter, that is where she will remain, preceded by all the descendants of the Princes Charles, Andrew and Edward. The line of succession therefore has to retreat by one generation and seek out other descendants of Queen Elizabeth's father.

Born on 21 August 1930 in the overpoweringly romantic setting of her mother's family home of Glamis Castle in Scotland, Princess Margaret Rose was the first immediate member of the royal family to be born north of the border since the future Charles I at Dunfermline in 1600. Whether or not she was breathed upon at birth by the unhappy ghosts of Macbeth and Bonnie Prince Charlie who are both said to have stayed in the same house, Margaret has not had an easy life as the Queen's younger sister.

With uncanny frequency in the recent history of the royal family, it is the monarch's second-born who has succeeded to the throne. But it was not so for Margaret, the second-born and last of the children of the Duke and Duchess of York, who six years after her birth were to be swept unwillingly to the throne as King George VI and Queen Elizabeth. It was Margaret's elder sister who ascended the throne on their father's death in 1952.

From that moment Margaret was destined to play a life's role as a second fiddle, a part for which she was ill-suited. For her there was no job, no obvious supporting role, nor did she give much indication that a supporting role to her sister was the kind of life she indeed wanted.

In the 1950s, when the bright young things still wore taffeta and wired bras, Margaret was the focus of London's 'In' set. She fell deeply in love with Group Captain Peter Townsend, a dashing RAF officer attached to the royal household as an equerry, and their desire to marry was mutual. But Townsend was divorced, and in that era the attitude of the English ruling class to divorce was as stiff as their underwear. The decision of the royal advisers that the Queen's sister could not

Above: holding court: Princess Margaret with friends on her holiday isle of Mustique.

Opposite: Princess Elizabeth grew up to love real horses — Princess Margaret did not.

marry a divorcé soured Margaret for years afterwards.

In the 'swinging Sixties', the most fashionable profession to follow was that of photographer, and Margaret duly married one, Antony Armstrong-Jones, who was rewarded with the title Earl of Snowdon. When that marriage in its time crumbled, attitudes to divorce had changed markedly; even the Queen agreed that, in the circumstances of domestic unhappiness, it was the right thing to do, and she took care to remain on the best possible terms with both parties.

Margaret's disappointment in life seemed to turn almost to bitterness, and she sought consolation among a tight circle of well-heeled friends on the tiny Caribbean island of Mustique, where she had been given a building plot as a wedding present. She kept up a minimum of public engagements, and on rare occasions was called upon to exercise her duties as a Counsellor of State, acting for the Queen while the monarch was abroad. But it was a minimal kind of role; at an early stage in the reign she had even been denied the chance to act as Regent in the event of her sister dying before Prince Charles reached his majority; the Queen assigned that role specifically to Prince Philip.

Some of those who saw her on official public display began to compare her unfavourably with other royal ladies like Princess Alexandra and the Duchess of Kent, who managed to conduct their royal engagements with all the necessary graciousness and charm.

As the mid-1980s approached and her own mid-fifties beckoned, Princess Margaret finally seemed to mellow somewhat, and to come to terms with herself. She took on more public engagements, and those who saw her at them remarked that she looked healthier and happier than for many years. But fate again took a hand, and early in 1985 she was admitted to hospital with a serious recurrence of bronchial trouble, doubtless exacerbated by a lifetime of cigarette-smoking.

10

Viscount Linley

David Albert Charles Armstrong-Jones, Viscount Linley, born on 3 November 1961, is a carbon copy of his father in looks and temperament.

The elder child and only son of the Earl of Snowdon and Princess Margaret prefers to be known as plain David Linley. He is the only member of the royal family to have made his way in the world using his hands, employing the creative talents he inherited from his photographer father. His parents had plans for him to go to Eton, but he went instead to Bedales, a lesser public school much favoured by the higher aristocracy. He then won a place at the distinguished John Makepeace School for Craftsmen in Wood, in Dorset, to learn furniture-making under one of the country's outstanding craftsmen.

After graduating from his two-year course Linley set up a cooperative workshop with a group of fellow students, at Dorking in Surrey, making one-off pieces which sold better to rich, novelty-crazed Americans than to the more conservative British. Perseverance has since brought him a healthier domestic order book.

He long ago fled the nest of his mother's apartments at Kensington Palace, although he keeps a room there; he prefers the flat near his workshop, where he can emulate the Bohemian life pursued by his father before marriage. Linley prefers the company of creative people to his royal cousins, although he is a close friend of Prince Andrew.

Among the Sloane set, Linley has something of a reputation as a ladies' man, and he is frequently seen at their smart parties. He is, however, determined to distance himself from Court circles, despite the fact that he is the only man alive who can legitimately address the British sovereign and head of the Commonwealth as 'Auntie'.

Viscount Linley, who inherited his father's subsidiary title – chosen to commemorate an ancestor, the cartoonist Linley Sambourne – will in due time inherit the earldom of Snowdon, but that alone will not relieve him of the need to work for a living. There are, however, more than enough young males ahead of him to ensure that his wish not to be involved in royal duties will be granted.

11

Lady Sarah Armstrong-Jones

The royal roadshow faces a future with a distinct shortage of princesses. Lady Sarah Frances Elizabeth Armstrong-Jones, younger child and only daughter of the Earl of Snowdon and Princess Margaret, and bridesmaid to the then Lady Diana Spencer, may well be called upon at some stage to fill the gap.

Lady Sarah, born on 1 May 1964, is the most senior royal female of her generation after the Princess of Wales, and must therefore be a strong contender to join the select troupe of performers who represent the monarch at official functions and thereby earn a place on the Civil List, with its not ungenerous payment of expenses from taxpayers' money.

She is widely liked by all the family, has remained a close friend of the Princess of Wales in an alliance of smart city-girl interests against the encircling green-wellington squirearchical bias of most of the royal family, and is a favourite of the Queen, who took a motherly interest in her and her brother after their parents' divorce.

Following royal tradition, Lady Sarah showed minimal academic talent at Bedales School, leaving with a solitary 'A' level but gaining a place at Camberwell Art School in south London. She cycled to Camberwell every day from her mother's apartments at Kensington Palace, and cultivated a regulation art-college scruffiness which could not entirely disguise the piercing blue Windsor eyes and an accent certainly not honed on the streets of Lambeth. After taking time off to follow her father on an assignment on the location set of David Lean's *A Passage To India*, she returned to college to specialize in textile design.

Lady Sarah prefers the company of creative and college friends to the Sloane set – although she has been seen at many a Sloane ball with the sort of upper-crust escorts such functions attract. She takes strongly after her much-adored father in temperament, but her physical appearance she owes largely to her mother. She has tried hard to bridge the gap of divorce between her parents, who separated when she was only 12, and maintains close relations with both.

The rules of title dictate that although her mother is a royal princess, Lady Sarah can inherit neither title nor position from her; she is Lady Sarah because her father is an earl. Her only route to higher station is through marriage.

Inset left: just the ticket: Lady Sarah Armstrong-Jones (right) arrives at a fancy-dress party with her cousin Edwina Hicks.

12

The Duke of Gloucester

Having run through all the living descendants of George VI, it is necessary to step back yet another generation, to George V. His first son, who reigned briefly as the ill-fated Edward VIII, had no issue, so after his second son George VI the line moves to his third son Henry, born in 1900 and created Duke of Gloucester.

Henry, who died in 1974, had two sons by his wife Alice Christabel Montagu-Douglas-Scott, a daughter of Scotland's largest private landowner the Duke of Buccleuch. The dowager duchess is still alive and active under the title of Princess Alice, Duchess of Gloucester.

Their elder son Prince William of Gloucester, a bright young career diplomat in the Foreign Office with a passion for flying and fast cars, would have succeeded to the title on his father's death had he not himself died tragically in a light aircraft accident in 1972 at the age of 30. The title therefore passed to his shy and studious younger brother, Prince Richard of Gloucester, who had never expected such a fate and had begun to build his own private career by qualifying in architecture at Cambridge University.

Richard, born on 26 August 1944 by Caeserean section when his mother was 42, spent his infant years in Australia where his father was governor-general. He was already practising as an architect in north London, known simply as Richard Gloucester, when his father died and he succeeded unwillingly to the title, being forced to abandon his chosen profession to become a full-time public figure, and proprietor of the family's 2,500 acre estate at Barnwell, Northamptonshire.

On his second day at Cambridge he met Birgitte van Deurs, a 19-year-old languages student, daughter of a Danish lawyer, whom he married in 1972 and who now finds herself Duchess of Gloucester. Known affectionately in the royal family as Proggy (Prince Richard of Gloucester), the retiring, bespectacled Duke dislikes alcohol and detests smoking, but admits to a weakness for chocolate. Among more than 50 organizations of which he is patron is ASH – Action for Smoking and Health – a militant anti-cigarette lobby.

Richard Alexander Walter George Windsor is entitled to style himself 'His Royal Highness', being the grandson of a monarch. He can trace a tortuous and somewhat indirect path of descent from his namesake Richard of Gloucester, Shakespeare's villainous hunchback who reigned briefly as Richard III.

The present Richard of Gloucester undertakes his share of official duties on behalf of the Queen. He has represented her at the independence celebrations of minor and distant colonies, presiding over the final dissolution of the British Empire. When not travelling abroad, the Duke divides his time between his splendid sixteenth-century family home at Barnwell, in the rich farmlands of Northamptonshire, and his grace-and-favour apartments at Kensington Palace. His high-speed dashes by car between the two have occasionally come to the attention of the police, but by contrast he will occasionally turn up at an official function in London on a motorcycle, his high breeding hidden inside the anonymity of a crash helmet.

The Duke and Duchess of Gloucester photographed by Norman Parkinson at their Northamptonshire home, Barnwell Manor, with labrador Tarqua and three Australian terriers. Barnwell, home of the late Prince Henry, Duke of Gloucester, is still occupied by his widow Princess Alice, Duchess of Gloucester, mother of the present Duke. The present Duchess is the former Birgitte van Deurs, daughter of a Danish lawyer.

13

The Earl of Ulster

Alexander Patrick Gregers Richard Windsor, Earl of Ulster, is the eldest child and only son of Richard, Duke of Gloucester, and his Danish wife Birgitte. Born on 24 October 1974, he will one day inherit the manor of Barnwell and the title Duke of Gloucester, but he will be a common or garden duke – if dukes can ever be common or garden – and not a royal duke like his father and grandfather. Except in the direct line of succession, the style 'Royal Highness' is inherited from the sovereign only for two generations, and dies with the death of the sovereign's grandson.

14

Lady Davina Windsor

Lady Davina Elizabeth Alice Benedikte Windsor, born on 19 November 1977, is the second child of the Duke and Duchess of Gloucester, and their elder daughter. She will suffer from the English custom of primogeniture, whereby the eldest son takes all, and will inherit nothing by right unless her father chooses to make specific provision for her in his will. She will remain 'Lady Davina' unless she chooses to upgrade her title by marriage to a man of higher station.

15

Lady Rose Windsor

Lady Rose Victoria Birgitte Louise Windsor, born on 1 March 1980, is the youngest child of the Duke and Duchess of Gloucester, and will share the same fate as her sister, with no rightful inheritance. But as a great-granddaughter of George V, she will not be without pedigree, or a topic of conversation at dinner tables. When the three Gloucester children grow up, it is unlikely that they will have any official or public role to play; by then there will be sufficient princes and princesses in line above them to fulfil all the demands of monarchy.

Snap: Alexander, Earl of Ulster, aged 6, son of the Duke and Duchess of Gloucester, rounds on a photographer equipped with camera, binoculars and water bottle.

Children of the Gloucesters: (l to r) Lady Rose Windsor, Alexander Earl of Ulster, Lady Davina Windsor.

The Duke and Duchess of Kent, photographed in their grace-and-favour London home at York House, St James's Palace, 1983 before setting out on a visit to the Middle East. The Duke travels widely promoting exports as vice-chairman of the British Overseas Trade Board.

16

The Duke of Kent

The Duke of Kent, along with his sister Princess Alexandra, occupies an unusual place in the royal family's close-woven genealogical web, for he is a cousin not only of the Queen, both being grandchildren of George V, but also of Prince Philip, through his mother Princess Marina, daughter of Prince Nicholas of Greece.

Kent is one of England's oldest dukedoms, first conferred by William the Conqueror on his half-brother Bishop Odo, but dormant for centuries until revived for the Duke of Kent who was Queen Victoria's father. The present Duke inherited the title from his father George, Duke of Kent, fourth son of George V.

Edward George Nicholas Paul Patrick Windsor was born on 9 October 1935. He was given the conventional education for someone of his rank, attending first Eton and then Sandhurst. In his subsequent career as a soldier, he distinguished himself in foreign languages, becoming a French interpreter in the Royal Scots Greys. His other military distinction was in skiing: he came tenth out of 146 competitors in the British Army of the Rhine ski championships in 1961.

After service in Germany and with the United Nations in Cyprus, the Duke retired from the Army in 1976 to pursue a career that is half business and half royal. He undertakes a number of official functions on behalf of the Queen, but his principal occupation is as vice-chairman of the British Overseas Trade Board, an active but suitably non-political body which promotes British exports. He is best-known for his presidency of the All-England Lawn Tennis Club; he and his wife present the trophies at Wimbledon every year. He is less well known in his position as head of the English Freemasonry movement, his title being Grand Master of the United Grand Lodge of England.

In 1961 the Duke married a commoner, the strikingly elegant Katharine Worsley, daughter of Sir William Worsley, a one-time colonel in the Green Howards and Lord Lieutenant of Yorkshire. The Duchess, who was educated at a private school in Yorkshire and an Oxford finishing school, shares with her husband the rota of royal engagements, and has her own substantial portfolio of patronages.

Although the Kents receive for their public duties a substantial Civil List allowance (£127,000 in 1985–86), they are among the less obviously wealthy members of the royal family. Unlike the allowances of the more senior members of the family, the Kents' income does not come from the taxpayer; in common with the allowances of the Gloucesters and Princess Alexandra, it is paid for by the Queen from her Privy Purse funds, drawn from the profits of her substantial landowning interests in the Duchy of Lancaster.

More obviously, the Kents have no lands or estate of their own. They sold the family home of Coppins, in the village of Iver, Buckinghamshire, and are now grace-and-favour tenants of the Queen at Anmer Hall, a large house on the Sandringham estate. They also have a grace-and-favour residence in St James' Palace known as York House, which was occupied by David Prince of Wales before his brief career on the throne as Edward VIII.

17

The Earl of St Andrews

George Philip Nicholas Windsor, Earl of St Andrews, was born on 26 June 1962, the eldest child of the Duke and Duchess of Kent. He showed early academic promise and was the first member of the royal family to become a King's Scholar at Eton. The talent faded temporarily, and he had to attend a cramming school to gain his university entrance qualifications, proceeding to Downing College, Cambridge, to study history. The Earl will have to make his own way in the world, his father having no great estates to pass on to him. He will, on his father's death, become Duke of Kent but, unlike his father, he will not be styled 'His Royal Highness', such title dying out with the present Duke, who is George V's grandson.

Lord Nicholas Windsor

Lord Nicholas Charles Edward Jonathan Windsor, born on 25 July 1970 as the second son and third child of the Duke and Duchess of Kent, will inherit even less than his elder brother. He is currently pursuing his studies at Westminster School, away from the public gaze, and can look forward to a life largely untrammelled by the trappings of royalty.

Above: children of the Duke of Kent at Windsor with their uncle and aunt Prince and Princess Michael: (l to r) George Earl of St Andrews, Lord Nicholas Windsor, Lady Helen Windsor.

Right: Lord Nicholas Windsor leaves Heathrow with his mother, the Duchess of Kent.

Lady Helen Windsor

Lady Helen Marina Lucy Windsor, born on 28 April 1964 as the second child and only daughter of the Duke and Duchess of Kent, had the distinction of being the first royal baby to use the surname of the British royal house. All those born in line before her had titles and therefore no need of such a lowly appurtenance as a surname.

Her distinguished family name has not prevented Lady Helen from slipping seven places in her lifetime to her current position in the line of succession. With Lady Sarah Armstrong-Jones, an almost exact contemporary, she shares the gossip-column limelight as the most glamorous of the peripheral royals, her ample figure having earned her the name of 'Melons' among the Sloane set.

After schooling at St Mary's, Wantage, Lady Helen finished her formal education as one of 20 girl sixth-formers in the robustly masculine environment of Gordonstoun, where she was a contemporary of Prince Edward. Academic achievement was not Lady Helen's forte: she managed a single 'A' level in art, and followed the course of many an upper-crust young lady of limited formal qualifications by joining a Bond Street auction house to learn about the art world. She went off to France after a short period, and returned to pursue the study of French at the Institut Français in London. She stands to inherit no further title from her family, and will remain Lady Helen unless she marries into higher station.

20

Lord Frederick Windsor

Logically, the twentieth position in the line of succession at present ought to be occupied by Prince Michael of Kent, grandson of George V and younger brother of the present Duke of Kent. But in 1978 Michael disqualified himself and renounced all rights to the throne by a simple and incontrovertible act: marriage to a practising member of the Roman Catholic Church.

His desire to marry Baroness Marie-Christine von Riebnitz, an Austrian distantly descended from some minor mid-European royalty, presented a double difficulty: the lady was not only a Roman Catholic, but had been previously married to an English banker, Mr Tom Troubridge. No one so close to the throne – Prince Michael was sixteenth in line at the time – had married a divorcée before, and by the 1702 Act of Settlement, designed to prevent a return to the throne of the Jacobite descendants of James II, anyone marrying a Catholic automatically loses his or her place in the succession. The ban was reinforced by the Royal Marriages Act of 1772.

It was a constitutional bramble patch. Prince Michael declared that he would willingly give up his constitutional rights, given that they were, in any event, largely theoretical. The Queen, after consulting the Privy Council, the Archbishop of Canterbury, and the Pope, eventually gave her unconditional consent to the marriage; but the Pope did not.

Divorce is not recognized by the Catholic church, but Mr and Mrs Troubridge had obtained a civil divorce in England, and the Catholic church had subsequently granted them an annulment. But the Pope refused remarriage in a Catholic church,

his objection being the declaration of Prince Michael, who is after all a cousin of the head of the Church of England whom he had no desire to embarrass, that any children of his proposed marriage would be raised in the Anglican faith.

The couple were eventually married at a civil ceremony in the town hall at Vienna on 30 June 1978; divorce barred them from a Christian ceremony in either a Catholic or a Protestant church, and a nineteenth-century legal quirk excludes members of the royal family from marrying in an English register office, those who drew up the law believing that no such exalted person would ever want to.

Michael and Marie-Christine spent their wedding night apart, so that the new Princess Michael of Kent could celebrate Mass with a clear conscience. The Archbishop of Canterbury blessed the union at a private ceremony four months later, and in 1983 Pope John Paul II finally relented and gave permission for the couple to receive the Catholic marriage rite, at a private ceremony in Westminster Cathedral.

Princess Michael's own parents divorced in 1950. Her father emigrated to Mozambique to run a fruit plantation, but his past returned to haunt his daughter in 1985, when much publicity was given to the fact that he had been a member of Hitler's SS; his precise role, however, remained unclear. Princess Michael's mother meanwhile went to Australia and married a Polish count. The Princess's maternal grandfather was the last Austro-Hungarian ambassador to Tsarist Russia, and her great-great-grandfather was Prime Minister of Austria-Hungary in the 1880s.

Prince Michael of Kent's marriage to the Austrian Roman Catholic divorcée Marie Christine von Riebnitz was the most controversial royal wedding for many years. Barred from either an Anglican or Catholic church wedding, and even from an English register office, they were married at a civil ceremony in Vienna town hall. Here the bride and groom pose after the marriage with the Duke of Kent, Princess Alexandra, Lady Helen Windsor, Princess Anne, Earl Mountbatten, and the Hon. Angus Ogilvy.

Such is the lineage of Lord Frederick Michael George David Louis Windsor, born on 6 April 1979, who, being brought up in the Anglican faith, takes his father's place in the line of succession. Lord Fred, as he is known to the family, has an unusual first name to add to his unconventional circumstances: Frederick fell out of favour as a royal name after the early death of 'Poor Fred',

George III's father, who was regarded as somewhat halfwitted.

Lord Fred, who divides his time between a London day school and his parents' Gloucestershire home of Nether Lypiatt Manor, near Stroud, will know little of such intricacies. He will remain on the outer fringes of royalty with no title nor position to inherit beyond his courtesy title of 'Lord'. Like his father, who is a director of Standard Telephones and Cables and three other City companies, he will have to make an independent career for himself.

Lady Gabriella Windsor

Lady Gabriella Marina Alexandra Ophelia Windsor, born on 23 April 1981, is, despite her highly ornamental nomenclature, in the same unprivileged position as her brother Lord Fred. The daughter of Prince and Princess Michael of Kent remains in the line of succession for the same reasons as her brother, but is too far removed from the throne to play any active part in the royal show.

Even her parents teeter on the very fringes of the royal act. They have been heard to complain privately that they receive no allowance from the Civil List, but the great majority of their public engagements are undertaken on their own account rather than on behalf of the Queen. The Prince, for example, is president of the Royal Automobile Club, and the Princess a trustee of the Breast Cancer Research Trust. Such honorary positions are strictly speaking no different from those occupied by a local mayor or Rotary Club president.

But if Ella, as Lady Gabriella is known, grows up with the forceful personality and elegant good looks of her mother, she should not have too much difficulty in making her way in the world.

Lord Frederick Windsor, son of Prince and Princess Michael of Kent.

22

Princess Alexandra

Princess Alexandra reached maturity just as her cousin Queen Elizabeth ascended the throne in 1952 and, because of the shortage at that time of young royal females, was quickly pressed into service assisting the new monarch with her round of public appearances, despite her relatively humble position in the succession.

She is the sister of the Duke of Kent and Prince Michael, the second child of Prince George (fourth son of George V), and of Princess Marina of Greece. She therefore shares with her brothers the unusual distinction of being a cousin of the Queen through her father, and of the Duke of Edinburgh through her mother.

Alexandra Helen Olga Christabel was born on 25 December 1936 and was five years old when her father was killed in a wartime flying accident. She was brought up by her mother at the family home of Coppins in Buckinghamshire and was the first British princess to experience a normal school education, at Heathfield girls' boarding school in Berkshire. This was followed by a spell at a Paris finishing school and a nursing course at the Hospital for Sick Children in London.

Princess Alexandra is immensely popular with her public, partly because of her natural elegance and unstuffy manner, and partly because many people still remember her mother with affection.

Being one step removed from the fulcrum of monarchy, she enjoys the luxury of a certain informality in her public appearances, which helps to break down the barrier of her towering six-foot frame. She is one of the hardest-working members of 'the firm' on official duties, and has made something of a speciality of representing the Queen at the weddings of distantly-related European royalty.

Alexandra was married in 1963 to the Hon. Angus Ogilvy, second son of the Earl of Airlie and a man with an impeccable Eton and Guards background who subsequently entered merchant banking and narrowly escaped some of the fringe bank collapses of the 1960s. Other, less prudent, public figures had their fingers badly burned.

The Ogilvys do not number themselves among the outstandingly rich of British royalty. They own Thatched House Lodge, a quite unstately residence in Richmond Park, and have a grace-and-favour apartment in St James' Palace, but Alexandra has no estates, and the Airlie lands have passed to Angus Ogilvy's elder brother.

Princess Alexandra has always shouldered a large burden of royal public duties, and is a particularly popular figure. Here she is seen in her drawing room at Thatched House Lodge, Richmond, before a state visit to Poland, and with winners of 'Children of Courage' awards at Westminster Abbey.

James and Marina Ogilvy with Princess Alexandra. Their father is in the Hunting Ogilvy tartan.

23

James Ogilvy

Of all the royal children, the Ogilvys lead the closest thing to private lives. Indeed, with the dedicated connivance of their parents they have grown up in virtual obscurity, almost entirely shielded from the public eye, and it is there they are likely to remain – in pursuit of relatively normal, if comfortable, citizenship.

James Robert Bruce Ogilvy, elder child of Princess Alexandra, was born on 29 February 1964, thirteenth in line to the throne, but he has slipped ten places in the meantime. He followed his father to Eton where he performed well academically, but not quite well enough to gain a place at Oxford. A spell at a high-class cramming school won him a place at St Andrew's University, much favoured as a second choice by those who just fail to make it to Oxford or Cambridge, and now with a reputation as a fount of right-wing economic philosophy. James, who has no title to inherit, is expected to follow his father into the City.

24

Marina Ogilvy

Marina Victoria Alexandra Ogilvy was born on 31 July 1966 as the second and last child of Princess Alexandra and Angus Ogilvy. Her life so far has been almost entirely private, although for a short time there were worries about her security from possible kidnap while she attended school at St Mary's, Wantage. She left school without any 'A' levels in 1984, and has been contemplating a career in art and design, possibly drawing some talent from her mother, who is a highly accomplished needlewoman. Like her brother, Marina may look forward to a life of relative obscurity, her fate being to appear at the edge of vast royal family group photographs and have the viewer puzzle, 'Who's that?'

THE
Lascelles

George, Earl of Harewood, at his family seat, Harewood House,
with his second wife, the former Patricia Tuckwell.

25

The Earl of Harewood

Imagine that, in the early years of this century, the suffragettes, as well as securing the vote for women, had taken their case further and altered the sexist provisions of the rules of succession so that the daughters of monarchs succeeded before the sons. We should now be ruled by King George VI – but a quite different one – and Queen Bambi. And the man who currently finds himself heir to the throne would be merely the Hon. Charles Mountbatten, son of Admiral and Lady Elizabeth Mountbatten.

The George VI in question would be George Henry Hubert Lascelles, 7th Earl of Harewood, elder son of George V's only daughter Mary, the Princess Royal. But as the rules of succession remain firmly in favour of the male line, George Lascelles and his family must be content to remain mere aristocrats who are so distant from the fulcrum of monarchy that they are not even considered members of the royal family. It is a position to which they do not raise the slightest objection.

George, Earl of Harewood, a future director of the Edinburgh Festival and of English National Opera, is held by his maternal grandmother Queen Mary at his christening in Yorkshire in 1923. He is flanked by his parents, Princess Mary and Viscount Lascelles, and his grandfather King George V. Among the godparents with the Archbishop of York in the back row is Prince George, Duke of Kent (3rd from r).

The Lascelles were one of those ancient Norman families who sailed for England in the wake of William the Conqueror, lured by the promise of rich pickings in the Frenchman's new domain. They journeyed to Yorkshire and settled near the modern town of Northallerton, where they dwelt for centuries in relative obscurity.

The family first achieved notice during the Civil War; a Lascelles served as a colonel in Cromwell's New Model Army and sat on the commission that tried Charles I. That particular Lascelles would have been mortified to know that one of his descendants would lie twenty-fifth in line to a restored British throne. A century later, the family had abandoned politics in favour of business. Henry Lascelles left Northallerton in 1739 and settled in Wharfedale, between the modern towns of Leeds and Harrogate, at a manor recorded in the Domesday Book of 1086 and known as Harewood.

Henry was not content to be a minor country squire; he travelled to the West Indies and acquired for himself the post of collector of customs on the island of Barbados, already one of the world's primary producers of rum, sugar and spices. As customs officers were apt to do in those days, Henry made himself a fortune in trade, buying sugar plantations and dealing, less salubriously but most profitably, in slaves.

With such wealth he was able to build himself a grand mansion back home in Wharfedale. Harewood House was begun in 1759, a Palladian country house built to the design of John Carr of York, with interiors by Robert Adam, furniture by Thomas Chippendale (a native of nearby Otley) and gardens by Capability Brown.

Harewood House remains the family home, although the present Earl lives there in circumstances much reduced from those of his ancestors. The sugar plantations are long since sold (although the family retained substantial holdings in the West Indies until well into the present century) and death duties have hit the Harewoods as hard as anyone else. George Lascelles lives in a small section of the house, well away from the public rooms through which the paying public wander, and his domestic staff is reduced to a cook, house-keeper and butler, and a live-in couple who do the cleaning.

It was the present Earl's father who established the royal connection. Henry Lascelles, 6th Earl, a dashing and well-connected Grenadier Guards officer, who had seen service in the First World War and been decorated with the DSO, married Princess Mary, only daughter of George V, at Westminster Abbey in 1922. He was 40 years old, and she 25. He had penetrated royal circles by becoming a personal aide-de-camp to the King, and went on to become lord lieutenant of the West Riding of Yorkshire, and chancellor of Sheffield University. The couple lived at Harewood, and Princess Mary, never one of the most glamorous royals, quietly and assiduously pursued a life of good works. They had two children, George and Gerald.

The family are well accustomed to life on the outer fringes of royalty. A cousin, Sir Alan Lascelles, was private secretary to George VI, and to the present Queen in the early years of her reign. The young George Lascelles, born in 1923, was a train-bearer at George VI's Coronation in 1937, and after war service as a captain in the Grenadier Guards (during which time he was wounded in Italy and captured as a prisoner of war) became aide-de-camp to the governor-general of Canada. He served as a Counsellor of State during the the monarch's absence abroad in 1947 and again during Queen Elizabeth's major post-Coronation Commonwealth tour of 1953–54.

But George Lascelles, schooled at Eton and King's College, Cambridge, in a manner somewhat untypical of his breed, has made an outstandingly successful career for himself in a field far removed from Court ritual. He has been director of the Edinburgh International Festival, managing director of Sadler's Wells Opera and of English National Opera, administrator of the Royal Opera House, Covent Garden, and editor of the magazine *Opera*. In 1985 he resigned from his day-to-day administration of the nation's principal opera company and retired to Harewood House to devote more time to running his stately home.

Lord Harewood has had a colourful personal life. In 1949 he married the exotically named Maria Donata Nanetta Pauline Gustave Erwina Wilhelmina Stein, known to her nearest and dearest as Marion, by whom he had three children: David, James and Jeremy. The marriage was dissolved in 1966; two years previously he had had

a son, Mark Lascelles, by Patricia Tuckwell, known familiarly as Bambi, an Australian divorcée whose brother, Barry Tuckwell, is one of the world's outstanding French horn virtuosi.

The Earl married Bambi in 1967, and their son was subsequently legitimized and granted the honorary title of the Hon. Mark Lascelles; but, being born out of wedlock, he has no claim to a place in the line of succession. The former Countess of Harewood, meanwhile, married the Rt. Hon. Jeremy Thorpe, one-time leader of the Liberal Party, who was later obliged to give up his parliamentary career after having his name drawn into a homosexual scandal.

George Lascelles, 7th Earl of Harewood, grandson of King George V.

26

Viscount Lascelles

David Henry George, Viscount Lascelles, eldest son of the Earl of Harewood and heir to his title and to Harewood House, was born thirteenth in line to the throne in 1950, but has since slipped badly.

David did not follow his father to Eton, but went instead to Westminster School, where he soon showed that he had inherited much of his father's artistic temperament. He proceeded to Bristol University with the intention of taking a degree in the history of art, but left before graduating, and instead departed on an expedition to Guyana to collect butterflies for the display cases of Harewood House. He became a photographer and film maker, travelling to India to record the lives of exiled Tibetans, and still earns his living by the camera from his home in Wiltshire.

Viscount Lascelles has also taken after his father in his less-than-conventional personal life. He had two illegitimate children Emily (born 1976) and Benjamin (born 1978) by Margaret Messenger, a laboratory assistant and daughter of a carpenter, whom he subsequently married, but not before being obliged to seek the Queen's permission under the Royal Marriages Act because of his lowly but nonetheless direct position in the succession.

27

The Hon. Alexander Lascelles

After his marriage to Margaret Messenger, Viscount Lascelles had two further children. Alexander Edgar, the elder, was born in 1980, and will one day inherit the title of 9th Earl of Harewood.

28

Edward Lascelles

Edward is the second legitimate son of David, Viscount Lascelles, and Margaret Messenger. He was born in 1982. Unlike his elder brother, the Hon. Alexander, Edward has no title whatsoever, being only the second son of a Viscount, and remains plain 'Mr'.

29

The Hon. James Lascelles

James Lascelles, born in 1953, is the second son of the Earl of Harewood and the former Marion Stein, and the brother of Viscount Lascelles. Being the second son of an Earl, he is entitled to call himself 'The Hon.', but does not stand to inherit the Harewood title or property.

James followed his elder brother to Westminster School, where his artistic inheritance manifested itself in a talent for music. James became, and

remains, an accomplished rock musician, and played for some time in a group called Global Village Trucking Company. He is best known, however, for his hippy marriage in 1973 to a 19-year-old American, Fredericka Duhrrson, when the two were sharing the then-fashionable drop-out life in a commune at Wortham, Norfolk. The groom wore a Tibetan wool jerkin, leather jeans and a green shirt, while the bride wore the satin and lace wedding dress of James' grandmother the Princess Royal. The couple, who have two children, have emigrated to the United States, and now live in New Mexico, where James pursues his musical career.

30

Rowan Lascelles

Rowan Lascelles, born in 1977, is the second child and only son of the Hon. James Lascelles and the former Fredericka Duhrrson. The male child takes precedence over his elder sister, but is too far removed from the direct Harewood line to take any title but 'Mr'.

31

Sophie Lascelles

Sophie Lascelles is the elder child of the Hon. James Lascelles and Fredericka Duhrrson, born in 1973 soon after her parents' hippy wedding in Norfolk. Like her younger brother Rowan, she takes no title.

The Hon James Lascelles, wife Fredericka, and children Sophie and Rowan at home in Suffolk.

32

The Hon. Jeremy Lascelles

Jeremy Lascelles, born in 1955, is the third and last child of the Earl of Harewood and the former Marion Stein. Like his brothers, he was educated at Westminster School; he followed his brother James into the rock music business, almost as soon as he left school, and since 1979 has been a recording executive at Virgin Records in London. Like his brother, he spends much of his life living down his royal connection and would much prefer to forget it. He married Julie Baylis in 1981.

33

Thomas Lascelles

Born in 1982, Thomas Robert Lascelles is the elder son of the Hon. Jeremy Lascelles, and a grandson of the Earl of Harewood. His parents are infinitely grateful that he takes no title, and can grow up a pure and unsullied commoner.

34

Ellen Lascelles

Ellen Lascelles, born in 1984, is the second child of the Hon. Jeremy Lascelles. She shares with her brother a lack of any title, and will be brought up by her father to ignore, as far as is humanly possible, her royal connection. In later years she may find it a source of mild amusement, but nothing more. She is currently the last of the descendants of the present Earl of Harewood and Marion, the first Countess.

35

The Hon. Gerald Lascelles

The Hon. Gerald Lascelles is the brother of the Earl of Harewood, the second son of Princess Mary the Princess Royal, and a grandson of George V. True to the family tradition, he has led a mildly unconventional life, deliberately distancing himself from any royal connection.

Born in 1924, Gerald followed his brother to Eton, but did not show quite the same degree of artistic talent. When he left school the war had begun, and he spent the first part of it toiling unglamorously in a munitions factory, although he subsequently found his way into uniform as a captain in the Rifle Brigade. A full-time military career did not, however, appeal: after demobilization Gerald went into engineering, taking a job with David Brown Tractors. For much of his life he has pursued a varied business career, dabbling in companies ranging from motor engineering to furniture manufacture.

His real interest has been motor racing; he became president of the British Racing Drivers' Club, and a director of Silverstone, and sponsored his own car on the circuits during the 1960s. An enthusiastic driver himself, he has been booked for a number of minor motoring offences on the public highway. His other consuming interest, which proves that the Harewood artistic flair survives in him after all, has been jazz, a subject on which he has become a considerable authority and a respected critic.

Gerald had one son, Henry, by his first wife Angela Dowding, whom he divorced in 1978 to marry an actress, Elizabeth Colvin, by whom he had had a son, Martin, in 1963. He now lives with his second wife near Cheltenham, Gloucestershire.

Almost his only connection with royalty was to

buy, in 1956, Fort Belvedere, the one-time home of Edward VIII before his abdication, where the feckless king would hold smart parties and leave his confidential State papers around for all and sundry to read; Stanley Baldwin, the Prime Minister, used to wonder why Acts of Parliament and secret Foreign Office cables came back to him covered in the ring-stains of martini glasses. Gerald sold the pile, on the edge of Windsor Great Park, to an Arab businessman in 1976.

The Hon Gerald Lascelles, a former president of the British Racing Drivers' Club, at work on the engine of a Mini in 1969.

36

Henry Lascelles

Henry Ulick Lascelles, born in 1953, is the only legitimate heir of the Hon. Gerald Lascelles. He married in 1979 but as yet has no children. With him, the line of succession therefore reaches the end of the descendants of George V, and the end of the blood line of the house of Windsor. George V's eldest son, Edward VIII, produced no children, nor did his youngest, the sickly Prince John who died in 1919 at the age of 13. We must therefore retreat one more generation, to George's father Edward VII, and then trace any living descendants of Edward's other children.

THE
Fifes

James, Duke of Fife, pictured on his Scottish estate in 1985.

Edward VII reigned as the only British monarch of the house of Saxe-Coburg, sandwiched between Victoria, last of the Hanoverians, and George V, who abandoned his patently German family name at the time of the First World War and took instead the name of his most historic official residence. Edward had six children, but only three produced heirs. His eldest son, Albert Duke of Clarence, predeceased his father, thus thrusting the second son George to the throne in 1911. Edward's second daughter Victoria died a spinster in 1935, and his youngest son Alexander John died at birth in 1871. The future George V was the only son to marry and have children, and the line of succession therefore passes next to Edward's eldest daughter, Princess Louise.

Princess Louise was born at Marlborough House in 1867, while her mother the future Queen Alexandra was in the midst of a severe bout of rheumatic fever. In 1889, at the age of 22, Louise married a rich Scottish landowner and astute businessman, Lord Macduff, who had also managed a brief career as a Liberal MP. It was not exactly an arranged marriage, but Macduff was a close friend of Louise's father, then still Prince of Wales, who did everything possible to encourage the courtship. Once the union had been effected the Prince of Wales pestered his mother Queen Victoria to grant Macduff a dukedom; the Queen thought it unnecessary and rather excessive, but eventually relented and made Macduff the 1st Duke of Fife. In addition to her title Duchess of Fife, Princess Louise, as her father's eldest daughter, assumed the title of Princess Royal when he ascended the throne in 1901.

King Edward adored his daughter and, with his mother dead and gone, heaped further honours upon her and her husband. Victoria had created

Macduff an ordinary duke, not a royal duke; in 1905 Edward went one better and granted the couple the privilege of allowing their children to bear the appellation 'Royal Highness'. He also ensured that Parliament voted Princess Louise a Civil List income of £6,000 a year.

The Duke and Duchess of Fife had two children. The first, Princess Alexandra, in a fine piece of royal inbreeding, married Prince Arthur of Connaught, son of Queen Victoria's third son Arthur. She took the title Princess Arthur of Connaught and gave birth to one son, Alastair Arthur, who in his turn became Duke of Connaught. He died without issue in 1943 and that particular lineage therefore came to an end.

The second of the Duke and Duchess of Fife's children was Princess Maud, born in 1893. In 1923 she married the 11th Earl of Southesk, Eton and Sandhurst educated and a major in the Scots Guards. Maud died in 1945 but at the time of writing the venerable Earl, aged 92, was still living at Kinnaird Castle, the old family seat of the Southesks situated near Brechin, in the rich farming country of north-east Scotland between Dundee and Aberdeen.

Maud and the Earl of Southesk had one son, James George Alexander Bannerman Carnegie, born in 1929. As the only surviving descendants of Princess Louise, Carnegie and his two children find themselves well up in the line of succession.

James Carnegie was educated at Gordonstoun, the school famous for its tough and supposedly character-building outdoor activities. He chose not to follow his father's military career, although he did find himself doing three years' national service in the Scots Guards in Malaya from 1948 to 1950. He chose instead to be a farmer, and studied at the Royal Agricultural College, Cirencester. Today he farms 1,500 mixed acres at Elsick, just north of Stonehaven, by the high and windy coast road that winds interminably over moor and cliff until it descends by a long hill into the grey northern city of Aberdeen.

On the death of the 1st Duke of Fife the title passed theoretically to his daughter Princess Arthur of Connaught, and on her death in 1959 it was assumed by her nephew James Carnegie, who is now 3rd Duke of Fife.

Shortly before he inherited his dukedom James Carnegie married into one of Scotland's great commercial families. The lady concerned was the Hon. Caroline Cicely Dewar, granddaughter of the 1st Baron Forteviot; the Baron's real name was Tommy Dewar, and he is immortalized on the label of one of the world's leading brands of Scotch whisky.

Along with James Buchanan, the proprietor of 'Black & White', Tommy Dewar took whisky from Scotland and sold it to the world. At the end of last century whisky was a drink little known outside its native land, and certainly not known by any brand names; if sold at all south of the border, it was generally in bulk from an anonymous cask. Pursuing the Englishman's taste for blended whisky, in which the heavy, heady Highland malts are cut with a lighter spirit, Dewar and Buchanan virtually founded the vast modern whisky industry with its profusion of brand names. Both became immensely rich, and both acquired titles, Buchanan becoming the 1st Baron Woolavington and Dewar the 1st Baron Forteviot. Their two companies eventually merged with a number of other leading producers to form what has become one of Britain's largest industrial enterprises, the Distillers Company.

Money, however, cannot buy happiness and

in 1966 the Duke of Fife's marriage to the whisky heiress was dissolved. The Duke, a freeman of the City of London and a former president of the Amateur Boxing Association, is now vice-president of the British Olympic Association.

38

The Earl of Macduff

David Charles Carnegie, Earl of Macduff, is the younger child and only son of the Duke of Fife, and heir to his title. David, born in 1961, was educated at Eton and Cambridge, and now lives in London where he works for a firm of City stockbrokers.

39

Lady Alexandra Carnegie

The elder child and only daughter of the Duke of Fife, Lady Alexandra Carnegie was born in 1959 and educated at Heathfield in Sussex. The prospectus of this fashionable girls' boarding school boasts: 'Few girls leave the school without having acquired the individuality and poise for which Heathfield is famous.' Individuality and poise have taken Lady Alexandra into the same career as the Princess of Wales before her marriage, that of a Montessori nursery school teacher. She too lives and works in London; at the time of writing neither of the Duke's children was married.

David Carnegie, Earl of Macduff, heir to the Dukedom of Fife.

Lady Alexandra Carnegie, daughter of the Duke of Fife.

THE
ROYAL HOUSE
OF
Oldenburg

Almost the entire Norwegian royal family assembles at the Royal Palace in Olso for the christening of Princess Martha Louise, daughter of Crown Prince Harald, heir to the Norwegian throne. The baby, although in line for the British throne, cannot succeed to that of her own country, where the constitution forbids the female line of succession.

Should the families of Windsor, Lascelles and Fife be annihilated at a stroke in some unimaginable holocaust, and should there nevertheless remain a nation to be governed, the British Crown would by rights be offered to the King of Norway, and it is conceivable that a new nation would then be created: the United Kingdom of Great Britain, Northern Ireland, and Norway.

The two nations are, of course, ancient allies, and the historic and cultural ties between Norway and Scotland are particularly strong. Indeed, Scotland's northern isles of Orkney and Shetland belonged to Norway until presented to the King of Scots as a marriage dowry in 1468. To this day in Shetland, almost every place name is Norse, and the nearest large city to the island capital of Lerwick is a close-run contest between Aberdeen and Bergen. For the current royal connection, however, we must return to Edward VII; his third and youngest daughter Princess Maud married a Danish prince who was destined to become the first king of an independent Norway for 500 years.

From the fourteenth century until 1814, Norway was little more than a province of Denmark, and was ruled throughout that half-millennium by the Danish Crown. But in that year the Danes, who had been allies of the then-discredited Napoleon Bonaparte, were forced to cede Norway to Sweden – a somewhat more natural union as the two countries form a single land mass and share a land frontier of over 1,000 miles. For the rest of the nineteenth century Norway was ruled by the kings of Sweden, the Swedish throne being occupied for much of that period by Oscar II. Norway was allowed a measure of independence, with its own government, armed forces, and civil service. In theory the two kingdoms were of equal status, but in fact the Swedes looked upon Norway as a province of their own country, and upon the Norwegians as a race of unsophisticated provincials.

The one area in which Norway was not permitted its own say was in foreign affairs, which remained in the hands of the king of Sweden. That in itself was an irritation to the Norwegians, but in 1885 they became thoroughly incensed when the Swedes democratized their own foreign affairs by taking them away from the king and putting them in the charge of a Council of State, but making no such provision for Norway. It was an affront to Norway's emerging sense of nationalism.

King Oscar II of Sweden, and of Norway until independence in 1905.

King Haakon and Queen Maud of Norway with the future King Olav V.

The Storting – the Norwegian parliament established at the time of union with Sweden in 1814 – had for long been in conflict with the monarchy over a wide variety of issues concerning Norway's freedom to act independently. The latest of these was a demand by the Norwegians that they should have their own diplomatic representatives to look after their interests abroad. One of the leading agitators for such a move was Fridtjof Nansen, the Norwegian polar explorer and scientist who rose to become one of the outstanding political figures of Europe as the nineteenth century drew to a close. Despite his association with Norway's case, and the worldwide respect that his name brought it, the Swedish Crown and government resolutely refused to allow Norway any say in its own foreign affairs.

In June 1905 the entire issue came to a head, and the Norwegian parliament resigned in defiant protest at the Swedish attitude. King Oscar of Sweden and Norway could find no politician willing to form another government, and the

Storting accordingly reconvened on 7 June, resolving that as there was no royal government, the constitutional royal power was in abeyance, and the union of the Crowns of Norway and Sweden was at an end. There were, for a brief period, rumours of war between the two nations, but diplomacy intervened and the tension was rapidly defused.

But what to do next? The creation of a Norwegian republic was briefly considered, and discarded; with the exceptions of France and Switzerland, Europe was at that time a solidly monarchist continent, and as the Norwegians' immediate reason for breaking up the union had been their desire for foreign representation, it was obvious that the newly-independent nation would need close contacts with the royal houses that formed the political reality of Europe at the time.

The Prime Minister of Norway remarked that the country was more likely to win friends abroad if it introduced a new member to the 'trades union of kings', and he went on to note that a crowned head

The future King Olav of Norway and his bride on honeymoon in England.

would be a more effective focus for the loyalty of the infant nation, well above the level of mere squabbling politics.

But where do you find a king when you have no royal house of your own? Quite simply, you have to import one. In what seemed a generous gesture of reconciliation, the Norwegians invited King Oscar of Sweden to nominate another member of his own family to be their king despite the exceedingly bad feeling that existed between the two countries at the time – a state of affairs not helped by Oscar being maddeningly slow in completing the formalities to renounce his Norwegian title. The invitation was no mere gesture, but a shrewd political gambit. The Norwegians prayed that Oscar would turn down the invitation – in fact he did not even bother to reply – but they knew that unless the Swedish royal house were given first refusal, no other European royal house would even consider an invitation, regarding it as bad form to muscle in on what had so recently been a Swedish domain.

With the Swedes clearly uninterested in having the throne of Norway back in the family, the Norwegians were free to make their own choice. This was narrowed down to Prince Carl, grandson of Christian IX of Denmark, and a nephew and son-in-law of Edward VII of Great Britain (first through the marriage of Carl's father to Edward's sister Princess Helena and second through Carl's own marriage to Edward's daughter Princess Maud). A major reason for the choice, apart from his excellent royal connections, was that Prince Carl, then aged 33, had a two-year-old son, Alexander, who would be a suitable Crown prince; the makings of a Norwegian dynasty were already there.

But first, the choice had to be approved by a referendum of the Norwegian people, who voted 259,000 to 69,000 in favour of the Danish candidate to their new throne. Prince Carl heard the result, on 18 November 1905, as he inspected a torpedo boat in Copenhagen harbour; he immediately accepted, and on the same day declared: 'I now assume the name of Haakon VII and give my son the name of Olav.' The two names were plucked from Norway's distant past, from the era of the Vikings and the Norse sagas.

The new King Haakon and his family sailed for Oslo, arriving in triumph despite a blinding snowstorm. Haakon VII was crowned in Trondheim Cathedral on 22 June 1906, the crown being placed on his head jointly by the Prime Minister and the Bishop of Bergen. It was the first Norwegian coronation, and the last; two years later the Storting, regarding it as too mystical and ritualistic, abolished the act of coronation. When Haakon's son Olav succeeded him in 1957, he too travelled to Trondheim Cathedral, but the service was one of consecration rather than coronation.

Although Haakon was elected by a large majority of the Norwegian people, he owed his position to no small extent to the machinations of Edward VII, who was after all his father-in-law. Edward suspected that, left to themselves, the Norwegians might have preferred a republic; in addition, he was well aware that the Emperor of Germany, Kaiser Wilhelm I, cherished hopes of placing one of his own younger sons on the Norwegian throne. Edward wished for neither outcome, preferring instead a soundly pro-British monarch on the throne in Oslo. He sent a wire to King Oscar of Sweden advising him not to oppose Prince Carl's nomination for the throne, and he implored Carl himself to accept the nomination, and to display the spirit of a king. Edward was hugely gratified when Carl was indeed elected.

Edward's daughter, Princess Maud, had become engaged to her first cousin Prince Carl of Denmark in 1895, in an age when royalty almost never married outside its own ranks. Carl, then an officer in the Danish Navy, was regarded as a good catch, and the couple were married at a quiet and private ceremony in the chapel of Buckingham Palace on

22 July 1896. Queen Alexandra, herself born a princess of Denmark, was delighted that her daughter had strengthened the Danish connection.

Haakon ascended a throne which had exceedingly limited constitutional power. He spent years as a somewhat anonymous cog in the Norwegian governmental machine, but was occasionally able to exercise his personal judgment, as in 1928 when to resolve a Cabinet crisis he brought his country's first Labour government into power. Queen Maud died in 1938, leaving Haakon to face a far greater crisis, and the bleakest years of his nation's history.

In the face of German invasion, and having refused to install a puppet government under the leader of the Norwegian Fascist Party, Vidkun Quisling – a man whose name passed into the language as a synonym for traitor – Haakon, Crown Prince Olav and members of the government left Oslo to seek safety up-country away from the German air raids. There then followed an astonishing eight-week manhunt through wild mountain country as the invaders pursued the King, often only hours behind him and clearly well-informed about his movements. At one stage he had to make a brief border crossing into Sweden to avoid capture; the carefully neutral Swedes were none too happy about it. To make matters worse, many of Haakon's own countrymen seemed almost reluctant to harbour him from the pursuing Germans.

Eventually the royal fugitives arrived in the far northern Arctic city of Tromsö where a British destroyer, *HMS Devonshire*, rescued them and took them to safety in Greenock, Scotland. Haakon brought to the Allied cause not only himself as a defiant figurehead against Nazism, but £63 million in bullion, almost the entire gold reserves of the Bank of Norway. In addition, he immediately dedicated the 1,000 ships of the Norwegian merchant navy to the Allied cause.

For much of the war Haakon lived at Foliejon Park near Windsor, and his tall, grizzled figure became a familiar sight in London as he travelled to town to do his shopping or to conduct the business of the government in exile. His refusal to accept German occupation, his resistance to calls from the puppet Storting for him to abdicate, and his defiant messages of hope broadcast from London, were a major contribution to the war effort; two-fifths of all the precious petrol brought into wartime Britain was carried in Norwegian tankers. Edward VII had shown remarkable foresight in pressing him to take the job in 1905.

Haakon's ceremonial return to Oslo in 1945 was a triumph for himself and his country. When he died in 1957, aged 85, he was greatly mourned in Britain as well as in his adopted homeland.

King Haakon and his Queen had only one child, born when he was still Prince Carl of Denmark and she was still Princess Maud. The boy was born at Appleton House, on King Edward's estate at Sandringham, on 2 July 1903, five weeks before Edward's coronation, and was christened Prince Alexander Edward Christian Frederik of Denmark. When Alexander was two years old, his father

A king becalmed: Olav at a yachting championship in 1961.

King Olav of Norway, still skiing at age 82.

accepted the throne of Norway; the boy automatically became Crown Prince of Norway, and was given the adopted Old Norse name of Olav.

Olav was barely out of his pram when he was introduced to affairs of State. He accompanied his father on the long journey across Norway from Oslo to Trondheim for Haakon's coronation. Although during his early years Olav received a private education at the hands of tutors, he was later sent to an ordinary secondary school, a decision made by his father for which he was forever grateful; Norway is a small nation of less than four million people, with no room for the rigid old class structure of the kind perpetuated by the British. He read science at school, and on graduating took a three-year course at the Norwegian Military Academy, officer training being an apparent prerequisite for the future monarchs of any nation. But Olav showed academic promise as well, and in 1924 he came to Balliol College, Oxford, to read political science and economics.

In accordance with the Constitution, when he reached the age of 18 Crown Prince Olav attended his first meeting of the Council of State, the regular Friday morning meeting between the King and his ministers at the royal palace in Oslo. The Constitution also requires that the heir to the throne should continue to attend regularly thereafter, to ensure that he is familiar with the workings of government and to avoid the mistake Queen Victoria made in not sharing the secrets of her high office with her son, the future Edward VII. When he was 23 Olav acted for the first time as Regent, or 'temporary executor of the royal power', while his father was abroad, in the same way that members of the British royal family act as Counsellors of State during the Queen's absence.

Olav of Norway on a state visit to Edinburgh in 1952 with the newly acceded Queen Elizabeth II.

When the royal party, fleeing from the invading Germans, arrived in Tromsö in June 1940, Olav volunteered to stay behind to organize the resistance movement while his father escaped to the safety of Britain. But he was persuaded that he could work more effectively abroad, and he became a tireless ambassador for the government in exile, travelling regularly to Washington to put his country's views to President Roosevelt, a man he greatly admired. As the appointed chief of the Norwegian defence forces, he was always on the alert, ready to lead a combination of resistance workers and Norwegian regulars trained in Britain and America, should action be required to dislodge the invader finally from Norway. In the

event, the total German capitulation rendered battle unnecessary.

Five days after the German surrender in Europe, Crown Prince Olav returned to Oslo, and in full battledress, riding high in an open car, drove through a city still far from safe from Germans and traitors. On 7 June 1945, the fifth anniversary of the royal family's flight from Tromsö, he welcomed his father the King back to a free Norway.

King Haakon's death in 1957 put Olav on the throne, and he remains only the second king of Norway this century. The Storting had abolished the ceremony of coronation in 1908, but the new King Olav V, although he needed only to swear an oath of allegiance to the Constitution, felt a strong personal need to have his accession marked in some religious manner. Accordingly he too journeyed to Trondheim, and on 22 June 1958, 52 years to the day after his father's coronation, attended a service of consecration in the same cathedral. Immediately afterwards he embarked on a grand tour to meet his people, travelling around the whole coast of southern Norway, and the following summer repeated the performance, touring the land of perpetual daylight in the far north of his immensely long kingdom.

King Olav has maintained the low-key approach of his father to his country's political life; he has been fortunate in not having had to face any major constitutional crisis, although his role has occasionally been questioned, and was debated in the Storting in 1976. It has been suggested in some quarters that as the entire family of King Olav, children and grandchildren, has married commoners, this may be creating an undesirable 'semi-nobility' made up of those associated with the royal house. At other times, the socialist left has claimed that succession by inheritance is unjust, although any doubts have always been directed at the institution, and not at the King himself. These questions having been fully aired, the Norwegian people appear content to retain a hereditary monarch.

One principle that might change one day, however, is that of Salic law, by which a woman may never accede to the throne and a search must be made for the dead monarch's nearest male heir, however distant he may be. It is a principle that has been common enough in Roman Catholic monarchies, but it sits ill in staunchly Protestant Norway, with its Scandinavian traditions of sexual equality and social progress.

While King Olav remains a discreet figurehead within his own country's constitution, he has always maintained a high profile elsewhere. For much of his long life he has been an outstanding sportsman, excelling in the twin Norwegian obsessions of skiing and sailing. When younger, he was a yachtsman of international renown. Given his own yacht when he was only 15, he went on to win a gold medal as a member of the Norwegian 6-metre class crew at the 1928 Olympics in Amsterdam. He has won sailing trophies throughout his life; even in 1971, at the age of 68, he took a bronze medal in the 5.5-metre world championships at Oyster Bay, Long Island, in the United States. He has been an Olympic sailing judge and a chairman of the Royal Norwegian Yacht Club, and is now honorary president of the International Yacht Racing Union. He still takes to the sea in the royal yacht *Norge*, a gift to his father from the Norwegian people after the war.

Olav has achieved distinction, although on a lesser scale, as a skier, and was competing at the terrifying Holmenkollen ski jump at Oslo when only 19; in a later contest at Drammen he missed the jump record by only 1½ metres. Like almost every other Norwegian, he has a winter mountain retreat, at Kongsseteren ('The King's mountain farm'), where he still takes to the slopes, although now in his eighties.

41

Crown Prince Harald of Norway

Crown Prince Harald, the youngest child and only son of King Olav and his wife Crown Princess Martha of Sweden, who died in 1954 after a long illness, is the heir to the Norwegian throne. His position would be usurped by his two elder sisters if Norway, which under its present constitution does not allow for a queen regnant, were to fall in line with Sweden, where the heir to the throne is now the monarch's eldest child irrespective of sex.

Such a change would not, however, alter Harald's position in the British line of succession, where the male still takes precedence over the female. Through his grandmother Queen Maud of Norway, a daughter of Edward VII of Great Britain, Crown Prince Harald is a second cousin of Queen Elizabeth. The close-knit web of European monarchy also makes him a second cousin of Queen Margrethe of Denmark, and a cousin of King Baudouin of the Belgians and Grand Duchess Josephine Charlotte of Luxembourg.

Crown Prince Harald was born on 21 February 1937 at Skaugum, the country estate outside Oslo given by a government minister to his father the then Crown Prince Olav as a wedding present in 1929, and subsequently passed on to Harald at the time of his own wedding.

When the Nazi armies invaded Norway in 1940, the three-year-old Harald fled with his mother and sisters to Sweden, while King Haakon and Crown Prince Olav travelled the length of Norway in their efforts to elude the invader. Crown Princess Martha and her children made their way overland across neutral Sweden to the Arctic port of Petsamo in Finland (now in the Soviet Union) from where a ship took them to the safety of the United States at the invitation of President Roosevelt.

The young Harald spent the five remaining years of the war at the Roosevelts' Pooks Hill property in Maryland, outside Washington DC, returning to share in his family's triumphant homecoming to Oslo in June 1945. During the German occupation it was commonly believed in Norway that the thrones of King Haakon and his son Olav, both in exile in England, had been lost but it was hoped that at some future time King Harald might be able to re-establish the monarchy. Those people rather under-estimated their reigning monarch, Haakon VII.

Back in his homeland, young Harald, in keeping with the Norwegian egalitarian tradition, was sent to ordinary state schools. Because European monarchs are, ex officio, head of their country's armed forces, all heirs to thrones seem obliged to undergo military officer training; Harald duly attended the Cavalry Officers' Candidate School and the Norwegian Military Academy. Between 1960 and 1962 he followed his father to Balliol College, Oxford, where he read economics, history and political science.

Heirs to thrones equally have to learn about government, a requirement which in Britain has no formal shape or pattern, but which in Norway is enshrined in the Constitution; Norwegian heirs are entitled, and expected, to attend the weekly Friday morning Council of State from the date of their eighteenth birthday, not to participate or to vote, but to listen. Crown Prince Harald has accordingly done so, between pursuing his duties as a representative of the Norwegian throne and people at home and abroad; he is undoubtedly the only member of any royal family to have visited the bleak and remote volcanic island of Jan Mayen, in the far north Atlantic between Iceland and Spitzbergen, which is Norwegian territory.

Harald's abiding passions, however, are the same as his father's: cross-country skiing and sailing; indeed there are few Norwegians who are

Crown Prince Harald of Norway studies the national flag.

and essentially secret romance which he spun out for nine years. The lady in question was Sonja Haraldsen, the daughter of a self-made Oslo businessman; she had been educated at Lausanne and Cambridge, and had read French and English at Oslo University.

As in Britain, the heir to the Norwegian throne must have the monarch's permission to marry. King Olav, realizing that marriage to a commoner would not only be controversial but could also raise constitutional issues, put the question to the Storting, the parliament in Oslo. Opinion was divided on the question of a commoner queen; Conservatives and Liberals did not mind, but the Labour Party, along with the centre-right Agrarian Party and the small Christian People's Party, was

Norwegian wood: young Harald learns the national obsession.

not obsessed with one, or the other, or both of these sports. A sailor since the age of ten, Harald has competed three times in the Olympic 5.5-metre class, in 1964, 1968, and 1972, although medals have unfortunately eluded him. He has been president of the Royal Norwegian Yacht Club and is on the committee of the International Yacht Racing Union.

Although in many ways appearing to be a solid traditionalist, Crown Prince Harald revealed himself as a revolutionary in 1968 when he announced his intended marriage to a commoner, the first time that any such thing had been proposed in the short history of the modern Norwegian monarchy. His grandfather had married the daughter of the king of Great Britain, and his father the daughter of the king of Sweden. Two British royal princesses, Margaret and Alexandra, had already married commoners, but neither princess had more than a wild outside chance of inheriting the British throne. What Harald proposed was extremely rare among the monarchies of Europe; he wanted to marry outside the club.

He was obliged to conduct a long, frustrating

Crown Prince Harald, heir to the throne of Norway created a precedent among European royalty in 1968 when he married a commoner, Sonja Haraldsen. A ten-year secret courtship culminated in a debate in the Norwegian parliament before the marriage was permitted.

not at all sure. The balance of opinion, however, was that no harm would be done, and a highly relieved Harald and Sonja were married in Oslo Cathedral in August 1968, Sonja taking the title of Crown Princess.

Harald, whose accession to the throne of Norway, in view of his father's age, cannot be far distant, is likely to continue the monarchy in its present style. Norwegian kings always appear to be on their best behaviour, partly because they are strictly and precisely governed by the Constitution, and partly because the nation, far less steeped in monarchical tradition than Britain, could easily opt for a republic instead. Kings Haakon and Olav were careful to adopt a relatively modest lifestyle, and always to act with exact constitutional correctness. The future King Harald may be expected to do the same.

42

Prince Haakon Magnus of Norway

Prince Haakon Magnus, born in 1973, is the younger child and only son of Crown Prince Harald and Crown Princess Sonja, and as such is the heir apparent to the Norwegian throne. Like his father and grandfather before him, he attends an ordinary Norwegian state school in Oslo, and his everyday life is not greatly different from that of his contemporaries. The Norwegian Crown, unlike the British, is not burdened by centuries of tradition and privilege. Haakon Magnus enjoys a life very different from that of Prince Charles at a similar age; he has no bodyguards, no public role to fulfil, and is relatively free from the intrusions of a press and public hungry for every crumb of gossip. Virtually his only reminder of his royal station occurs on Sundays, when King Olav regularly invites all his grandchildren living in the Oslo area to a grand family dinner at the Royal Palace; these reunions are known as 'grandfather's dinners'.

43

Princess Martha Louise

The elder sister of Haakon Magnus, and only daughter of Crown Prince Harald, Princess Martha Louise was born in 1971, and like her brother attends a normal state school in Oslo.

She was named Martha after her grandmother Crown Princess Martha of Sweden, and Louise after King Olav's grandmother and great-grandmother, who were respectively queens of Denmark and Sweden. But Martha Louise will never be Queen, unless Norway changes its constitution in line with that of Sweden and declares that the first-born, irrespective of sex, shall inherit the throne.

Prince Haakon Magnus and Princess Martha Louise of Norway.

44

Princess Ragnhild

When Princess Ragnhild Alexandra was born in Oslo in 1930, the eldest child of King Olav (then Crown Prince Olav), she had the distinction of being the first royal child born in Norway since the Middle Ages. Twenty-three years later she made further history, by being the first princess of any European reigning royal house in living memory to marry a commoner. Because she was a woman, and therefore not in line for the strictly male Norwegian throne, the union caused much less disquiet than did that of her younger brother Crown Prince Harald some years later.

Her husband was Erling Lorentzen, a Norwegian shipowner who had been in the Resistance during the German occupation, and whom she had met on the day that her father returned to Oslo in triumph after the war, when she was a member of the royal party and he of the military escort.

She now enjoys the somewhat arcane distinction of being the leading resident of South America in line of succession to the British throne. Her husband moved his shipping business to Rio de Janeiro soon after their marriage, although the family make frequent return visits to Oslo.

Princess Ragnhild's son Haakon Lorentzen is unquestionably the only Brazilian hang-gliding champion ever to have been in line of succession to the British throne. The eldest grandson of King Olav, Haakon was born in Oslo in 1954 and, besides his fascination with hang-gliding, has the usual Norwegian obsession with competitive sailing. He spent his childhood in Brazil, studied business administration in the United States, and then worked for a year in a Norwegian bank before returning to Rio to join his father's shipping business. In 1982 he married a Brazilian Roman Catholic, Martha Freitas, and has therefore disqualified himself from the British succession.

His sister Ingeborg Lorentzen was born in 1957, the second child and elder daughter of Princess Ragnhild. She too was educated in Rio, trained as a pre-school teacher, and in 1982 married a Brazilian Roman Catholic lawyer, Paolo Ribeiro. Her aunt, Crown Princess Sonja, and her cousin Princess Martha Louise went to Rio for the wedding. The couple now live in Oslo, where Paolo is an importer-exporter specializing in trade between his own country and his wife's ancestral homeland. Her marriage to a Roman Catholic, however, has ruled Ingeborg out of the British succession.

45

Ragnhild Alexandra Lorentzen

The youngest child of Princess Ragnhild, her mother's namesake, is the only one of the family born in Brazil, in 1968, and the only one still eligible for a place in the British line of succession. She is still at school in Rio, but makes frequent visits to Oslo, including one in 1983 for her confirmation service in the royal palace in the presence of King Olav.

Haakon Lorentzen's marriage ruled him out of the succession.

Crown Prince (later King) Olav with his wife Crown Princess Martha and their three children Princess Ragnhild, Prince Harald and Princess Astrid, pictured in 1937. Olav's marriage to Martha, a member of the Swedish royal family, healed the rift between the two houses created by Norway's declaration of independence.

Princess Ragnhild, daughter of King Olav, who married Norwegian businessman Erling Lorentzen and went to live in Rio de Janeiro. Ragnhild has remained on the sidelines of Norwegian royalty; her sister Princess Astrid acted for a time as first lady of Norway on the premature death of their mother Queen Martha.

46

Princess Astrid

Princess Astrid Maud Ingeborg is the second daughter of King Olav, born in 1932 and named after her aunt, Queen Astrid of Belgium, and her two grandmothers, Queen Maud of Norway and Princess Ingeborg of Sweden. She was only eight years old when the Germans invaded Norway, and she was forced to flee with her mother and sister to the United States. She returned to Oslo in 1950 to finish her schooling and came to England for two years to take a degree in English literature at Lady Margaret Hall, Oxford.

She was only 22 when her mother, Crown Princess Martha, died. Her newly-wed sister Ragnhild having departed to Brazil the previous year, and her brother the future heir to the throne being still unmarried, Astrid found herself the only woman member of the royal family, and was immediately thrust into the position of first lady of Norway.

Her royal duties increased still more when her already-widowed father ascended the throne in 1957; she accompanied him as his escort on official tours at home and abroad, and played hostess to a succession of visiting foreign heads of State. For a time her private life had to take second place, but in 1960 – the year in which both Princess Margaret, and King Baudouin of the Belgians, broke new ground by marrying commoners – she received her father's consent to marry a close friend of long standing, Oslo businessman Johan Martin Ferner. Astrid had become well known during her years of acting as virtual Queen of Norway, and foreign royalty was well represented at her wedding at Asker, near Oslo, in 1961.

With the heir to the throne still unmarried, Princess Astrid had to continue in her public role for another seven years until Crown Prince Harald's marriage – also to a commoner. But she still found time to have her first three children. Two more children followed soon after Harald's marriage. As soon as she was able to hand over the major burden of her official duties Astrid renounced her annual State allowance of 50,000 kroner – about £5,000, a mere pittance by the standards of the British royal family's Civil List allowances. She and her husband continue to live at Asker, in a relatively modest home given by King Olav as a wedding present. Her place in the limelight has long been taken by her brother's wife, the future Queen of Norway, Crown Princess Sonja.

Princess Astrid, daughter of King Olav, who married a commoner Johan Ferner, in 1961.

All in line; the five children of Princess Astrid of Norway.

47

Alexander Ferner

The elder of the two sons of Princess Astrid, born in 1965, Alexander Ferner is training for a business career in Norway. After graduating from the Oslo Business School in 1984, he joined a firm of Oslo ship brokers as a trainee. In his final months at the business school, as a member of the students' council, he was at Fornebu airport at Oslo to welcome Princess Diana on a visit to Norway – a few days before she announced her second pregnancy – and to present her with a huge bunch of carnations.

48

Carl-Christian Ferner

The younger son of Princess Astrid, born in 1972, is still a pupil at a state school near his home at Asker. Like all the monarch's grandchildren out of the direct line of succession, he is a commoner and takes no title.

49

Cathrine Ferner

The eldest child of Princess Astrid, born in 1962, left school in 1980 and has not yet been able to decide what to do for a living. She has floated from one short course to another, and at the time of writing was attending a Norwegian dressmaking school.

50

Benedikte Ferner

The second daughter of Princess Astrid and Johan Ferner, born in 1963, is a rather more purposeful lady than her elder sister. After attending school at her home at Asker she came to England to improve her English at a Cambridge language school, and is currently living in London where she is studying business at the London School of Foreign Trade.

51

Elisabeth Ferner

The youngest daughter of Princess Astrid, born in 1969, is still at school at Asker in Norway. Like her brothers and sisters, she is a commoner with no special position or privileges, who can walk down an Oslo street entirely unrecognized and unremarked. She does, however, have one distinction of which she may not even be aware; in the line of succession to the British throne, she is the last of the descendants of Edward VII, and will remain so until she herself has children.

THE
ROYAL HOUSE
OF
Hohenzollern

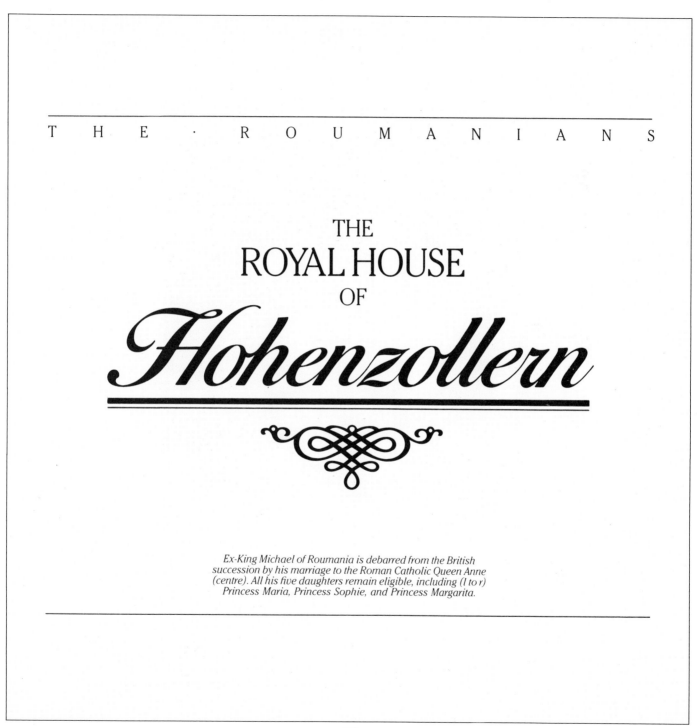

*Ex-King Michael of Roumania is debarred from the British
succession by his marriage to the Roman Catholic Queen Anne
(centre). All his five daughters remain eligible, including (l to r)
Princess Maria, Princess Sophie, and Princess Margarita.*

Having accounted for all the descendants of Haakon VII of Norway and his wife Queen Maud, daughter of Edward VII, we have exhausted all Edward's living descendants, and to find the continuation of the line of succession we must revert another generation to his mother, Queen Victoria.

Edward was Victoria's second child, but her eldest son; we must therefore look next to her second son Alfred, Duke of Edinburgh, born in 1844 and the second holder of the dukedom currently held by Queen Elizabeth's husband. Alfred married into the close-knit circle of European royalty; his chosen bride was Grand Duchess Marie of Russia, daughter of Tsar Alexander II. The wedding was a lavish affair at St Petersburg, attended by Alfred's brother the Prince of Wales, and the highlight of the celebrations was a boar hunt in which 80 beasts were shot by the visitors and their Imperial Russian hosts. The couple returned to live at Clarence House, London; Marie argued endlessly that, as the daughter of the Tsar, she ought to have precedence over the Princess of Wales at Court, but Queen Victoria would have none of it.

Alfred and Marie had six children, including one still-born daughter. The first was their only son, Alfred, who died young and left no heirs. Their second child and eldest daughter, also named Marie, is the one responsible for trailing the British line of succession through the short-lived monarchy of Roumania. Princesses in those days were expected to marry Princes, and these were in plentiful supply in the profusion of minor north European states that were welded together to form the nation of Germany. Marie found her prince at Sigmaringen, in the southern state of Württemberg. Prince Ferdinand was a scion of the great Imperial house of Hohenzollern. Marie was slender, tall and elegant, while Ferdinand was, on the contrary, a ponderous, slow-witted individual with gigantic jug ears. But Ferdinand's most important attribute was that his uncle Carol was King of Roumania.

Roumania was one of the shorter-lived of Europe's monarchies and, whatever else its kings might have been renowned for, stability and longevity did not figure high among their collective virtues.

The modern state was created in the aftermath of the Crimean War, when the east European principalities of Moldavia and Wallachia were made semi-independent provinces within the Turkish Empire, which had long held suzerainty over them. They had been independent states in the distant past; Wallachia numbered among its medieval rulers the dreadful Vlad the Impaler, widely held to be the real-life model for Bram Stoker's fictional creation, Count Dracula.

In 1859 the two provinces joined together and elected as their king a minor Moldavian prince, Alexander Cuza. He was not a notable success; his dissolute lifestyle and lack of leadership did not appeal to the new Roumanians, and they chased him out in 1866. They would not have another such prince, they decided, but would import an established and reliable brand of royalty. They approached the King of the Belgians, but he was unwilling to supply any of his family. So they turned to the Hohenzollerns, who provided Carol I.

Carol's wife was Elizabeth of Wied, better known as a writer of fairytales under the name of Carmen Sylva. The couple had one child who died in infancy, and Carol therefore nominated his nephew Ferdinand as his successor.

Carol was decidedly pro-German, but when King Ferdinand and Queen Marie succeeded him in 1914, within weeks of the outbreak of the First World War, all that changed. Queen Marie, being of English birth and upbringing, ensured that Roumania entered the war on the side of the Allies; the Roumanian army was rapidly routed, and the royal family had to flee to safety near the Russian border, where the Queen became a nurse.

Marie was a most determined woman, anxious perhaps to make up for her good, dutiful and much-loved but somewhat ineffectual husband. She arrived at the Versailles peace negotiations in 1919, the only woman present, and startled the assembled political heads of Europe with her dashing style: she took a 20-room suite at the Ritz, and installed herself with a wardrobe containing 60 gowns, 31 coats, 22 pieces of fur, 29 hats, and 83 pairs of shoes. Afterwards she made a grand tour of America, to become one of the most exotic and dazzling socialites of the flapper age. When King Ferdinand died in 1927 she went into virtual retirement, and died in 1938.

Ferdinand and Marie had six children, several of whom died without issue. The eldest son, Carol, was the obvious heir to the Roumanian throne; their daughter Marie married into the Yugoslav royal family, and reappears later in this book.

King Ferdinand and Queen Marie at their coronation in Bucharest, 1922.

Carol, however, grew up to be an absolute bounder; even George V said so. His fatal weakness was for women. In 1918, having taken to heart the socialist teachings of his Swiss tutor, he renounced his claim to the throne and ran off to marry Zizi Lambrino, a colonel's daughter, in the Russian Orthodox cathedral at Odessa. His furious parents very quickly engineered for the marriage to be annulled, but not before Zizi was carrying her short-lived husband's child. Their son, also calling himself Carol of Roumania, now lives in London and is much-married, with two children from two separate unions. Because of the uncertain legal standing of his parents' marriage, this particular Carol and his offspring must be regarded as disqualified from the succession.

Our other Carol, having had his marriage to Zizi forcibly annulled, then wed the beautiful and long-suffering Princess Helen, daughter of Constantine I of Greece. Theirs too was a brief union, although again it produced a son, Michael, this time of undoubted legitimacy. Carol soon fell for a flame-haired mistress of Jewish background, Elena Lupescu. Once again he eloped, renounced his claim to the throne, and took up residence with Elena in Paris. He was the great delight of the gossip columnists, and the despair of his family and the Roumanian government. When his father Ferdinand died, Carol's six-year-old son, Michael, was proclaimed King, under the care of a three-person Regency.

But Roumania was in the throes of economic and political crisis, with a sore need for firm leadership. Swallowing its pride, the government invited Carol to return, provided he left Elena behind. He accepted with alacrity, and took the throne in 1930.

In the meantime, however, Carol had obtained his divorce from Princess Helen of Greece. Despite all his promises to the contrary, he soon installed his mistress Elena in the royal palace in Bucharest just as though she were Queen. The notably anti-

King Ferdinand and Queen Marie of Roumania arrive at Dover for a state visit to England in 1924.

Semitic Roumanians put up with this affront for some time, because Carol was proving to be an effective leader of the nation. But he became increasingly dictatorial, and in 1940, at the undoubted instigation of Hitler, pro-Nazi elements within his own government deposed him, and chased him and his Jewish mistress out of the country. Carol and Elena wandered the world, were eventually married in Rio de Janeiro in 1947, and

King Carol of Roumania and Crown Prince Michael en route to lunch with the Lord Mayor of London, 1938.

retired to Portugal, where Carol died in 1953 and where Elena lingered on, lonely and impoverished, until her death in 1978.

Carol's son Michael was 19 years old when he assumed the throne for the second time, in 1940. He inherited a nation which had become embroiled in the Second World War on the side of Hitler, and which went on to fare exceedingly badly, with large losses of territory to the Soviet Union on the Eastern Front.

King Michael found himself little more than a figurehead in his own country, with all real power concentrated in the hands of the Fascist Prime Minister and virtual dictator, Ion Antonescu. In 1944, with the tide of events in Europe beginning to turn, King Michael took the exceedingly bold step of dismissing Antonescu, withdrawing from the war, and seeking an alliance with Stalin which he hoped would guarantee the security of his battered nation. The Russians agreed, but rapidly reneged

on their pledge, turning on the Roumanians and capturing over 100,000 of their officers and men. Within a year there was a Communist government in Bucharest.

For the time being, King Michael was permitted to remain in office, a tribute to his great personal popularity. But in 1947, returning from the wedding of Philip Mountbatten and Princess Elizabeth in London, he was told bluntly that he could either abdicate or face bloodshed in Roumania. He left for good, and the present-day Roumanian Peoples' Republic was born in the wake of his departure.

In 1948 ex-King Michael married Princess Anne, daughter of Prince René of Bourbon-Parma and Princess Margrethe of Denmark. Because the Princess was a Roman Catholic, Michael became ineligible for the British line of succession, as did Prince Michael of Kent in similar circumstances. But the couple have five daughters, all of the Protestant faith, and all in the line of succession.

After his abdication ex-King Michael lived for a while in England, but he is now based in Lausanne, Switzerland, where he pursues a quiet business career representing a number of European and American firms. Although still technically claiming his right to the Roumanian throne, he does not pursue it actively and makes few public pronouncements on the subject.

Michael's eldest daughter is Princess Margarita of Roumania, born in Lausanne in 1949. Her godparents include the Duke of Edinburgh and King Constantine of Greece. She spent her earliest years in England before going to school in Italy and Switzerland, and studying art in Florence. In 1970 she returned to Britain to take up a place at Edinburgh University, where she was awarded an honours degree in sociology.

Princess Margarita has achieved some eminence in the field of medical sociology, and her research work has been published in the *British Medical Journal* and other learned publications. After graduating from Edinburgh she carried out postgraduate research into the nursing profession, and more recently worked on a major international research project which studied the effects of alcohol on the widely differing cultures of Scotland, Zambia and Mexico. Her work has involved her in research projects for the World Health Organisation and for several UN agencies.

Currently living back at home in Lausanne, Margarita regards Scotland as her second home, where she can enjoy fishing, bird-watching, and rummaging in the junk shops of Edinburgh – always on the lookout for anything Roumanian.

She and her sisters in fact descend twice from Queen Victoria. In addition to the route just traced, they also descend through their grandmother, King Carol's wife Helen of Greece. Victoria's eldest daughter, Victoria the Princess Royal, married the German Kaiser Frederick III; their daughter Sophie married Constantine of Greece, and their daughter in turn was the Helen who married Carol.

Exile: Ex-King Michael, his wife and daughters Helen, Irene and Margarita on holiday in Denmark in 1954.

53

Princess Helen of Roumania

Like her elder sister, Princess Helen was born in Lausanne (in 1950) but spent her infant years in England, where her father was living after his abdication. She too went to school in Italy and Switzerland, but returned to London to pursue a career as a teacher of handicapped children, working at the Frances Holland School and at the London Academy of Music and Dramatic Art. She subsequently changed direction and took a two-year course in art restoration.

In 1983 Princess Helen married Professor Robin Medforth-Mills, a Fellow of the Centre of Overseas Research and Development at Durham University. Professor Medforth-Mills is currently on secondment to the United Nations and, although the couple have a house outside Durham, they have spent most of their married life so far in the Sudan, working among the Ethiopian refugees who have flooded across the border.

Professor Medforth-Mills has initiated a population studies centre at the new Sudanese university of Gezira, and the Princess has set up an international primary school adjoining the university. She has become closely involved with the UN's work on population, and in 1984 attended the World Population Conference in Mexico City. Recently the couple have embarked on a project to train 45 handicapped Ethiopian refugees in work such as printing, bookbinding and leathercraft, which should generate some income for them.

54

Nicholas Medforth-Mills

Princess Helen and Professor Medforth-Mills had their first child in 1985, a boy whom they have styled Nicholas Michael de Roumanie-Medforth-Mills. Born to Protestant parents, he takes his place in the line of succession.

55

Princess Irina of Roumania

The third daughter of ex-King Michael was born in 1953 in Lausanne, and was schooled in Switzerland and England. Since then she has worked on a stud farm in Canada, looked after handicapped children in Switzerland, worked at Christie's, the London auctioneers, and taken a secretarial course in Oxford. In 1984 she married John Kreuger, a Swede living in the United States, and they now breed horses and cattle in Oregon.

Princess Irina of Roumania at her wedding to John Kreuger.

56

Michael Kreuger

Princess Irina and John Kreuger had their first child in 1985, a son whom they have christened Michael Torsten Kreuger. Like his cousin Nicholas, born in the same year, he enters the line of succession.

57

Princess Sophie of Roumania

The fourth daughter of ex-King Michael was born among the Greek side of her family in Athens in 1957 and, like her sister Princess Irina, attended school in Switzerland and England. After school she worked for a short period as a nurse in England, but has since become a freelance artist; her paintings have been exhibited in the United States, the Bahamas, and in various countries of Europe. She recently embarked on a full-time course in fine art and photography at the University of North Carolina.

58

Princess Maria of Roumania

The fifth and last child of ex-King Michael was born in Copenhagen in 1964, and went to school in Switzerland and England. She took her 'A' levels at an English school in 1983 and, with the intention of becoming a nursery teacher, went to study at the Norland Nursery Training College in Berkshire. She marks the end of this particular branch of Queen Victoria's descendants, but to continue the line we need not regress very far: only to her paternal great-grandparents, King Ferdinand and Queen Marie.

THE
ROYAL HOUSE
OF
Karadjordjevic

The Balkan connection; Alexander I of Yugoslavia is married to Marie, daughter of Ferdinand of Roumania and a great-granddaughter of Queen Victoria. Alexander was the first to take the title King of Yugoslavia, in 1929, but he was assassinated by a Macedonian terrorist in Marseilles in 1934. He was the father of the last Yugoslav king, Peter II, and of Prince Tomislav, now an English apple grower. Marie died in 1961, and is buried at Frogmore, near Windsor Castle.

Young Prince Peter of Yugoslavia (centre) with his twin brothers, right Prince Philip and left Prince Alexander.

From Roumania, the line of succession now moves to Yugoslavia. The second daughter of King Ferdinand and Queen Marie of Roumania, also named Marie, married into the Yugoslav royal house in 1922; but the Yugoslav monarchy goes back a little further than that.

The modern state of Yugoslavia is an uneasy amalgam of disparate Balkan states created in the aftermath of the First World War, and even today the tensions between its different peoples occasionally bubble to the surface. Its short-lived monarchy sprang from the ruling dynasty of Serbia, which in turn had its origins in the early nineteenth-century peasant revolts against the Turkish occupation of the Balkans.

Two rival peasant families, the Karadjordjes and Obrenovics, led various insurrections against the Turks from 1804 onwards, and each enjoyed brief and alternating careers as princes of Serbia. The reign of the Obrenovics came to a final and abrupt end in 1903, when the Serbian army burst into the royal palace in Belgrade and assassinated the last Obrenovic, Alexander of Serbia, together with his highly unpopular wife. Their bodies were thrown out of a window on to the lawn, and the soldiery were entertaining themselves with gay abandon until the Russian ambassador suggested that it might be more seemly to remove the corpses.

*Prince Paul (right), Regent from 1934 to 1941 for Prince Peter,
grandfather of the present Prince Peter, opposite.*

Wishing to restore the rival Karadjordje dynasty, the Serbians recalled the head of the family, an old soldier living in relative poverty in Geneva. They provided a triumphant welcome for him in Belgrade, and crowned him King Peter I of Serbia. He reigned until 1914 when, aged 70 and in poor health, he stepped down in favour of his son Alexander. It was the young Alexander who, in the years immediately following the First World War, found himself the first monarch of the new kingdom of Yugoslavia, which was welded together from the states of Serbia, Slovenia, Croatia and Montenegro and from other Balkan fragments of the dismembered Austro-Hungarian Empire.

Holding the new nation together proved almost impossible; indeed it was said that the only true Yugoslav was Alexander himself. In a desperate effort to keep his kingdom together he dismissed Parliament and ruled as an absolute monarch.

Alexander I's father, although proud of his peasant origins, had married into the outer fringes of minor European royalty: his wife Princess Zorka of Montenegro numbered among her sisters the Queen of Italy and two Russian grand duchesses. But it was Alexander himself who really provided the link with the mainstream of European monarchy: in 1922, at Belgrade, he married Marie, second daughter of Ferdinand and Marie of Roumania, and great-granddaughter of Queen Victoria. She is now buried in the British royal family vaults at Frogmore by Windsor Castle.

The marriage was a happy one, but it ended abruptly in 1934 when Alexander, on a State visit to France, was assassinated in Marseilles by a hired gunman working for a Croatian terrorist organization; Alexander's efforts to mould Yugoslavia into a single nation still had a long way to go. His eldest son Peter was only 11 at the time of the shooting, and the country was put in the care of a Regency under Alexander's cousin, Prince Paul.

Prince Paul was exceedingly pro-British, having studied at Oxford University and married Princess Olga of Greece, the sister of Princess Marina who became Duchess of Kent. But when the Second World War came to the Balkans in 1940 with the Italian invasion of Greece, Prince Paul was faced with an appalling dilemma. Yugoslavia, surrounded by nations that had thrown in their lot with Hitler, militarily unprepared, and with no hope of assistance, decided that capitulation to the Nazis was the lesser of two evils, the greater being the threat of domination by Stalinist Russia.

Prince Paul therefore reluctantly signed a pact with Nazi Germany and Italy in March 1941. It was a highly unpopular move with the Yugoslav army, which revolted only two days later, abolished the Regency, and installed King Peter II, still six months short of his eighteenth birthday. Peter was crowned in Belgrade amid scenes of great rejoicing, but Hitler did not wait to discover the new regime's attitude to the war. Peter had been king for only nine days when the Luftwaffe attacked Belgrade.

Ten days later, Yugoslavia surrendered. King Peter had already fled the country, seeking brief respite in Athens and Alexandria before attempting to set up a government-in-exile in Jerusalem, in the heart of British-mandated Palestine. It was something of a farce, and before long the British had flown him to London, where he installed himself in Claridge's Hotel and based his government-in-exile at the Yugoslav Embassy.

Peter rapidly gained his wings with the RAF, and went up to Clare College, Cambridge. He wanted to be parachuted back into the Balkan mountains to lead the resistance movement, but the British would not permit it. It was the beginning of a widening rift between the Yugoslav King and the British government. Churchill, who began the war by backing the royalist Cetniks who were conducting resistance in Yugoslavia, ended it by giving wholehearted support to comrade Tito's rival band of Communist partisans. He was clearly

King Peter of Yugoslavia inspects a Guard of Honour on Hampstead Heath, 1942.

The engagement of Crown Prince Alexander of Yugoslavia and Princess Maria Gloria of Orleans Braganza is blessed at a Serbian Orthodox Church in Kensington.

unimpressed by King Peter and his ability to maintain stability in post-war Yugoslavia; there was also, undoubtedly, a desire to please Britain's ally in the east, Stalinist Russia.

By the end of the war King Peter knew that his cause was lost, particularly when, in 1945, Churchill stood up in the House of Commons and said in effect that the British government did not really give a damn about who ruled Yugoslavia. Nevertheless, when in 1945 a son and heir was born to Peter and his wife Alexandra, daughter of the King of Greece, the entire government-in-exile was summoned to the birth at Claridge's, and a

formal statement was issued, declaring that the infant was the true heir to the throne.

The infant was Crown Prince Alexander, who today would be restored to the throne of Yugoslavia in the unlikely event of that country's return to a monarchy. His father, King Peter, was finally dethroned by the Communists in November 1945, and the nation embarked on the post-war era still riven by internal racial differences but maintained in uneasy cohesion by the forceful leadership of Marshal Tito.

By the end of the war the private finances that the Yugoslav royal family had brought with them to

England had more or less run out, and King Peter was forced to abandon his suite at Claridge's for the more prosaic surroundings of the Yugoslav Embassy. After the war he lived for a time in France, then in the United States, attempting to regain some of his fortune by financial speculation. But it all went wrong; the ex-King turned increasingly to drink, and he died in Denver, Colorado, in 1970 at the age of only 47.

Crown Prince Alexander travelled with his family to the United States in 1948, and began his schooling in New York. For his secondary education he returned to Europe and had a spell at Le Rosey in Switzerland before attending Millfield public school in Somerset. In 1960 he enrolled at Culver Military Academy in the United States, and subsequently passed out from the Royal Military Academy, Sandhurst, as a serving British army officer in the 16/5 Queen's Royal Lancers.

When his father died in 1970, Alexander chose not to take the title of King. He said at the time that to do so would have had no constitutional effect, and indeed might cause friction. Besides, as a serving British army officer, it would have been inappropriate for him to make any kind of political declaration. He attended a memorial service for his father in London, but has since remained discreetly out of the limelight.

Crown Prince Alexander, who is descended from Queen Victoria through both his father and his mother Queen Alexandra of Greece, although much more directly through the former, removed himself from the British line of succession at a stroke in 1972 when he married a Roman Catholic. Although the couple subsequently separated and obtained a divorce, the marriage has debarred Alexander for life from the British succession.

The lady in question was his fourth cousin once removed, Princess Dona Maria da Gloria, elder daughter of Prince Dom Pedro of Orléans and Braganza, and a descendent of the last emperor of Brazil. They were married at a magnificent ceremony at Villanmanrique de la Condesa, near Seville, in the presence of many European royals including Princess Anne, who acted as principal witness for Alexander. The newlyweds emigrated to Brazil, where Alexander worked as an investment broker, but since their divorce he has returned to London as the European public relations representative of Wigham Poland, an American insurance company.

Crown Prince Alexander and Princess Dona Maria had three children, all of whom despite their Catholic mother were baptized in the Eastern Orthodox faith. Prince Peter of Yugoslavia, born in America in 1980, is the eldest, and will one day become Pretender to the Yugoslav throne if he so wishes. He has stayed with his father since his parents' separation and has been attending Hill House pre-preparatory school in Knightsbridge, where Prince Charles was once a pupil.

60

Prince Philip of Yugoslavia

Twin sons were born to Crown Prince Alexander and Princess Dona Maria in 1982, in Washington, DC. Although they have been living with their Roman Catholic mother since their parents' separation, both were baptized in the Orthodox faith in the same church in Spain where their parents were married. Philip is the elder twin by some minutes.

61

Prince Alexander of Yugoslavia

Alexander is the younger twin. He, like his brothers, is eligible for the British line of succession by virtue of his Orthodox baptism.

62

Prince Tomislav of Yugoslavia

Deep in the lush rolling downland of West Sussex, down a remote country lane near Billingshurst, is an apple orchard, and by the roadside is a farm shop where the produce is on sale. The man behind the counter is tall, dark and perfectly English-looking, and he speaks with a neutral English accent that bears virtually no trace of his native tongue. He is Mr T. K. George, farmer; he is also Prince Tomislav of Yugoslavia, brother of the late King Peter, who came to school in England in 1936 when his native land was still a monarchy, and has remained here ever since. He and his family long ago anglicized the name of the royal house of Karadjordje to 'K. George'.

Prince Tomislav sells the produce of his Sussex orchard.

Tomislav was born in Belgrade in 1928. He was already at school in England when war broke out and the Nazis invaded Yugoslavia. He went on to study economics at Cambridge, but gave up his course to work in a school for backward children, where one of his duties was to tend the garden. He took enthusiastically to the outdoor life, and shortly afterwards found himself a job as a farm labourer at Faversham in Kent.

When, in 1945, General Tito took over the post-war government of Yugoslavia, and King Peter was finally dethroned, it was clear that Prince Tomislav would never return. In 1950 he bought his West Sussex farm, and has remained there ever since, in a rambling, comfortably chaotic house which is full of royal mementoes and portraits. A good-humoured realist, Tomislav makes no pretence of working towards a return of the Yugoslav monarchy, but he is active and well-connected among the 20,000-strong Yugoslav émigré community in England.

His first marriage was to Grand Duchess Margarita Alice Thyra Viktoria Marie Louise Scholastica, a member of the royal house of Baden and a niece of the Duke of Edinburgh. Their wedding in 1957 was at Salem in Bavaria, near the Baden family seat, where the young Prince Philip had a brief and unfortunate period of education in 1933 at Kurt Hahn's original school which by then had fallen into Nazi hands. The couple were divorced after having had two children, Nikolas and Katarina.

Soon after his divorce in 1982 Prince Tomislav married his secretary, Linda Bonney, then aged 33, at the only Serbian Orthodox church in Britain, St Prince Lazar's in Bournville, Birmingham. By his second wife he has one son, George K. George, born in 1984.

Prince Tomislav of Yugoslavia marries secretary Linda Bonney at a Serbian church in Birmingham

63

Nikolas K. George

Nikolas Karadjordje, anglicized as Nick K. George, is the elder child and only son of the first marriage of Prince Tomislav of Yugoslavia. He was born in 1958 and went on to attend Box Hill School in Surrey, a spartan establishment on the Gordonstoun model. He has not, however, employed his expensive education, and now works as a labourer on a farm near that of his father.

64

George K. George

George, born in 1984, is the only child of the second marriage of Prince Tomislav. He was christened with due ceremony in the Serbian Orthodox rite in London, earning himself a photograph on the Court and Social page of *The Times*. He is being brought up by his parents on their Sussex farm.

65

Katarina K. George

Katarina is the second child and only daughter of the first marriage of Prince Tomislav. She too has anglicized her Serbian royal surname to K. George; she too attended Box Hill School. She sold furniture at Harrods and now works in public relations for a London publisher.

Princess Katrina of Yugoslavia, seen here aged 21, works in public relations in London.

66

Prince Andrej of Yugoslavia

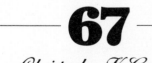

Prince Andrej is the youngest of the three sons of Alexander I, who ruled Yugoslavia from 1914 to 1934 and whose wife Marie provided the British royal connection for their children. Andrej's eldest brother ruled as King Peter, and his second brother is Prince Tomislav.

Andrej was born in Yugoslavia in 1929. Like Tomislav, he was sent to London to be educated and, because war intervened, never returned to his native country. After studying agriculture at Cambridge he bought a farm close to his brother's in Sussex, but did not survive the experience long. He returned to London but eventually settled in Portugal, a country that has always been something of a magnet for dispossessed European royalty. He now lives in Palm Springs, California, with his third wife the former Mrs Mitsi Lowe, a much-married American lady of distant Yugoslav roots. The Prince is a prominent Rotarian, and travels widely around the Pacific as a representative of Rotary International.

Prince Andrej has no children by his third wife, but the four offspring of his previous marriages are listed below.

67

Christopher K. George

Christopher is the only son and younger child of Prince Andrej's first marriage to Christina of Hesse, eldest daughter of Prince Christoph of Hesse and through that connection a niece of Prince Philip, Duke of Edinburgh. Christopher, born in London in 1960, is a British army officer.

68

Vladimir K. George

Prince Andrej's second wife, whom he married in Tunbridge Wells, Kent, in 1963, is Kira Melita Feodora Marie Viktoria Alexandra, a member of the princely house of Leiningen, and a granddaughter of Grand Duke Kiril Vladimirovich of Russia. Kira is herself descended from Queen Victoria; her grandmother was the daughter of Alfred Duke of Edinburgh, Victoria's son, and Marie of Russia. Vladimir, born in 1964, therefore descends from Victoria through both parents.

69

Dimitrye K. George

The second and last child of Prince Andrej and Kira of Leiningen was born in London in 1965, and shares the antecedents of his brother. In the same year that he was born, his parents adopted a child, whom they named Lavinia, but she cannot be included in the British line of succession, because birth within wedlock is an essential qualification for a claim to the throne.

70

Maria Tatiana K. George

Maria is the elder child and only daughter of Prince Andrej's first marriage. Also born in London, in 1957, she was briefly looked after by her great-uncle Prince Philip at Buckingham Palace at the time of her parents' divorce in 1960. Maria now works as a photographer in Los Angeles.

THE
IMPERIAL HOUSE
OF

Some of the many surviving Hohenzollerns of Prussia pose for a family group in 1984. They include Prince Christian (far left), Prince Michael (4th from left), Princess Marie Cecile (7th from left at rear) and Prince Georg Friedrich (on the knee of his grandfather Prince Louis Ferdinand).

71

Grand Duke Vladimir of Russia

The custodian of the Romanov throne.

With Maria Tatiana K. George, we exhaust the eligible descendants of Marie, the eldest daughter of Alfred, Duke of Edinburgh, Victoria's second son. The line therefore moves to Alfred's second daughter Victoria Melita, born in Malta in 1876, and brings the Imperial Russian house of Romanov directly into the British succession. As we have already seen, the British and Russian royal houses had already been united by Alfred's marriage to Marie, daughter of Tsar Alexander II. The two houses were shortly to be united again in a marriage which skirted uncomfortably close to the incestuous.

Victoria Melita was married first to a nobleman from the bottomless reservoir of minor German royalty, Ernst Ludwig, Grand Duke of Hesse. But it was an unhappy union which soon ended in divorce. Her eye then lighted on her first cousin Kirill, the son of her mother's brother Vladimir; the two were married in 1905 at Tegernsee in southern Bavaria.

Grand Duke Kirill immediately fell foul of his cousin Tsar Nicholas II, a small, weak, indecisive man who was destined to be the last ruler of Imperial Russia. Nicholas was infuriated, not because his cousin had married a close relative, but because a member of his Imperial family had married a divorced woman without the Tsar's consent. Kirill and his new bride were banished, but they did not stay out of the country for long; they were back in St Petersburg to witness events which lead to the 1917 Revolution.

In the early years of their marriage, Kirill and Victoria Melita, who was now known as Victoria Feodorovna, had two daughters – one in Germany and one in Paris, of whom more later. As the revolution gathered momentum in Russia during the spring of 1917, Victoria was pregnant with her third and last child.

Tsar Nicholas provided yet another connection with the British royal family, as his wife the Tsarina Alexandra Feodorovna was the daughter of Queen Victoria's second daughter Princess Alice. But their royal connections were to prove no defence whatsoever against communism. Nicholas and his entire family were subsequently murdered by the Bolsheviks at Ekaterinburg (now Sverdlovsk), although a great question mark hangs over the fate of his daughter Anastasia. Among those who died was Nicholas's only son Alexis, a sufferer from the haemophilia that has occasionally surfaced among Queen Victoria's descendants.

Grand Duke Kirill had a luckier fate; he escaped the pursuing Bolsheviks by fleeing with his pregnant wife across the ice into Finland, then still a part of the Russian Empire. He was the most senior member of the Romanov Imperial family to escape and survive. His wife Victoria gave birth to their only son Vladimir at the little town of Borga, near Helsinki, on 30 August, 1917.

For the first three years of Vladimir's life, the family lived as fugitives in Finland, constantly in fear of being discovered by the Bolsheviks and with scarcely enough food or wood to light a fire. The family eventually made their escape, and lived variously in Germany, Switzerland and the south of France before settling at St Briac, near Dinard on the north coast of Brittany.

It was there, in 1922, that Grand Duke Kirill, who had been a rear-admiral in the Imperial Russian Navy, proclaimed himself head of the Imperial House of Romanov, and subsequently added the title Emperor and Autocrat of All the Russias. When he died in France in 1938 his son Vladimir immediately assumed the position of head of the Imperial House of Romanov, which he still retains. Vladimir issued a manifesto in which he declared that following his father's example he assumed all the rights and duties which belonged to him by

Kira and Maria soon after their arrival in Paris as exiles.

The marriage of Prince Louis Ferdinand and Grand Duchess Kira of Russia at Doorn, Holland, in 1938. Kneeling by the bride is her brother Grand Duke Vladimir, current pretender to the Russian throne, while behind the couple, surrounded by a forbidding trio of Valkyries, is the ageing Kaiser Wilhelm II, who died three years later.

Grand Duke Vladimir bows to Metropolitan Eulogios at a Russian exiles' gathering in Paris.

virtue of the fundamental laws of the Russian empire and the statutes of the imperial family. He declared that he would style himself His Imperial Highness Grand Duke Vladimir of Russia, although other Russian emigrés were already swearing allegiance to him as emperor. He is a first cousin once removed of the last tsar, Nicholas II.

Grand Duke Vladimir was educated in Paris, but shortly before the outbreak of the Second World War he came to England, and studied briefly at the London School of Economics. In 1939 he began work in an engineering factory at Stamford, Lincolnshire. He had returned to St Briac for a holiday when war broke out and spent most of the war under virtual house arrest there. In 1944 he was deported to Germany, and then to Austria.

It was rumoured that while he was in Germany he had been approached by emissaries of Hitler who proposed that he return to a puppet throne in Russia, but he has always denied that any such contact ever took place. Although no friend of Stalin, Grand Duke Vladimir was implacably opposed to Hitler's attempts to invade and conquer Soviet Russia.

In 1946 Grand Duke Vladimir went to live in Madrid, where he still has a house, but he now spends the greater part of his time at the family home at St Briac. His life's work has been to keep alive the flame of Russian monarchy and his notepaper bears the crest of the Imperial Russian eagle. He has travelled widely to promote his cause; in 1985 he was back in London as guest of honour at a reception to launch the Russian Monarchist League.

In 1948 he married Leonida, the daughter of a Georgian prince from Tiflis, whose first husband, an American, Sumner Moore Kirby, died in a German prison. The couple have a daughter Maria.

72

Grand Duchess Maria of Russia

Her Imperial Highness the Grand Duchess Maria of Russia is the only child of Grand Duke Vladimir and has been named by him as his successor, a move which has not been universally welcomed by the Russian monarchist community. Despite the noble precedent of Catherine the Great, they are not all happy that the next head of the Romanov family should be a woman.

Maria, who will be styled according to her father's wishes as curatrix of the throne, was born in Madrid in 1953, and was educated at the English school there. At the age of nineteen she came to England to read Russian at Oxford University, although she did not stay to complete her degree course. In 1976, in a civil ceremony at Dinard near the French family home and subsequently at a Russian Orthodox service in Madrid, she married Prince Franz Wilhelm, a nobleman of the Prussian royal family and a man 10 years her senior.

The couple recently divorced, and Maria has returned from Madrid to live at the family home at St Briac. A difficulty, which Franz Wilhelm was never fully able to resolve, was whether he was a Russian or a Prussian. The Romanov family expected him, on his marriage, to act as Prince Consort to Grand Duchess Maria, and gave him the title of Grand Duke Michael of Russia. Franz Wilhelm, a law graduate, never took easily to the role, and eventually returned to the bosom of Prussian nobility.

The current Grand Duchess Maria of Russia at her wedding to Prince Franz Wilhelm.

73

Grand Duke George of Russia

Grand Duke George is the only child of Maria and Franz Wilhelm, who since his parents' separation has lived with his mother at the St Briac home of his grandfather, Grand Duke Vladimir. George was born in Spain in 1981, and baptized into the Orthodox faith at a service in the Greek Embassy in Madrid. Being Grand Duke Vladimir's only grandson, he can in due time expect to become heir to the Russian throne in succession to his mother. It is entirely possible, of course, that on reaching adulthood he will regard Russian monarchy as a lost cause, and will renounce the claims so carefully nurtured by his grandfather. Such a move would not, of course, affect his admittedly lowly position in the British line of succession.

74

Prince Emich of Leiningen

The line now moves to Vladimir's two sisters, both of whom have been dead for many years. The elder was Grand Duchess Maria of Russia, born in Germany while her parents, Kirill and Victoria Melita, were living out their brief banishment from St Petersburg. Maria was ten when her family fled from the Bolsheviks in 1917.

She married into the princely German family of Leiningen, the same family Princess Victoire, Queen Victoria's mother, had come from. Maria and her husband, Prince Karl, lived in the Leiningen Palace, the family seat at Amorbach, set deep in the hills that skirt the beautiful Rhine valley in southern Germany, high above Mannheim and Heidelberg. They had three sons and three daughters. Prince Karl was sent by the Nazis to fight on the eastern front and died in a Soviet prisoner-of-war camp in 1946. Grand Duchess Maria died five years later at the age of 44. Their eldest son is Prince Emich of Leiningen, born in 1926; he is married to the daughter of another German noble family, Her Highness Duchess Eilika Stephanie Elisabeth Thekla Juliana of Oldenburg. The couple have four children.

75

Prince Karl-Emich of Leiningen

Prince Karl-Emich, the eldest son of Emich and Eilika, was born in 1952. In 1984 he married Her Serene Highness Princess Margarita of Hohenlohe-Oehringen. The couple are the present occupants of the Leiningen Palace at Amorbach, where Queen Victoria's mother once lived and where she installed one of the first water-closets to be used in Germany.

76

Prince Andreas of Leiningen

The second son of Prince Emich and Princess Eilika was born in 1955, and is married to Her Royal Highness Princess Alexandra of Hanover.

77

Prince Ferdinand of Leiningen

His Serene Highness Prince Ferdinand, born in 1982, is the son of Prince Andreas and Princess Alexandra.

78

Princess Melita of Leiningen

Princess Melita, born in 1951, is the eldest daughter of Prince Emich and Princess Eilika. She is not married.

79

Princess Stephanie of Leiningen

The younger daughter and last child of Prince Emich and Princess Eilika, Princess Stephanie was born in 1958. She too is unmarried.

80

Prince Karl of Leiningen

Prince Karl, born in 1928, is the second son of Vladimir's elder sister, Grand Duchess Maria of

Russia. He married Princess Marie-Louise, of the deposed Bulgarian royal family, but is now divorced.

81

Prince Karl Boris of Leiningen

Prince Karl and Princess Marie-Louise of Bulgaria had two children. The elder, Prince Karl Boris, was born in 1960.

82

Prince Hermann of Leiningen

Prince Hermann, born in 1963, is the younger son of Prince Karl and Princess Marie-Louise.

83

Prince Friedrich of Leiningen

Prince Karl's brother and the third son of Grand Duchess Maria of Russia, Prince Friedrich was born in 1938. He has been married twice, but has no children.

84

Princess Kira Melita of Yugoslavia

Princess Kira, born in 1930, is the eldest daughter of Grand Duchess Maria of Russia. In 1963, at Langton Green near Tunbridge Wells in Kent, she married the divorced Prince Andrej of Yugoslavia (see no 66). The two children of the marriage appear at 68 and 69, their descent from Queen Victoria being more direct through their father than their mother.

85

Princess Mechtilde of Leiningen

Princess Mechtilde, born in 1936, is the youngest daughter of Grand Duchess Maria of Russia. Maria's middle daughter, Princess Margarita, born in 1932, is married to a Roman Catholic and is therefore disqualified from the succession. Princess Mechtilde is married to a German commoner, Karl Anton Bauscher, and lives at Bamberg in West Germany.

86

Ulf Bauscher

Ulf, the eldest of three sons of Herr Bauscher and Princess Mechtilde, was born in 1963.

87

Berthold Bauscher

The second son of Herr Bauscher and Princess Mechtilde, Berthold was born in 1965.

88

Johan Bauscher

Johan Bauscher, born in 1971, is Princess Mechtilde's youngest child; he completes the descendants of Grand Duchess Maria of Russia.

Prince Louis Ferdinand of Prussia and Grand Duchess Kira of Russia pose with their children for a 1956 family group. Those currently in the British 100 are Christian Sigismund (far left), Michael (2nd left), Friedrich Wilhelm (rear right) and Marie Cecile (front right). An extended list would include the other three: Xenia, Louis Ferdinand Jr. and Kira.

Prince Friedrich Wilhelm of Prussia

The line now moves to the descendants of Grand Duchess Kira of Russia, the youngest child of Grand Duke Kirill and Victoria Melita. Kira was born in Paris in 1909. She was eight years old when the family went into hiding in Finland.

Kira became well known in England before the war, when she came to London to act as bridesmaid at the wedding of the then Duke of Kent and Princess Marina of Greece. She was a first cousin once removed of the bride. The Prince of Wales, later Edward VIII, had begun his unsuitable association with Mrs Wallis Simpson by then, and

there was some thought, and even speculation in newspapers, that Grand Duchess Kira would be an infinitely more suitable match for the Prince than Mrs Simpson, but it came to nothing.

Several years later Kira married Prince Louis Ferdinand, head of the royal house of Prussia, in Orthodox ceremonies at Potsdam and at Haus Doorn in Holland. Within a year of their marriage war had broken out. The Prussian royal family kept their distance from Hitler, and Prince Louis Ferdinand narrowly escaped imprisonment and possible execution for being implicated in the so-called 'July Plot' to assassinate the Führer. After the war Kira and Louis Ferdinand lived at Bremen; she died in 1967, allegedly from shock at hearing that her eldest son proposed to marry a commoner.

The son, Prince Friedrich Wilhelm of Prussia, born in 1939, did indeed marry the commoner, Waltraud Freydag, but the marriage ended in divorce. He has since married Ehrengard von Reden, of a minor German noble family.

Prince Friedrich Wilhelm of Prussia, eldest son of Prince Louis Ferdinand, head of the old German ruling house of Hohenzollern. He is seen here with his second wife Princess Ehrengard, three-year old son Friedrich Wilhelm, and baby Viktoria Luise, pictured at her christening in 1982.

90
Prince Philip of Prussia

Prince Philip, born in 1968, is the only child of Prince Friedrich Wilhelm's marriage to Waltraud Freydag.

91
Prince Friedrich Wilhelm Jr.

Friedrich Wilhelm, born in 1979, is the elder son of Prince Friedrich Wilhelm's marriage to Ehrengard von Reden.

92
Prince Joachim Albert of Prussia

Joachim, born in 1984, is the younger son of Prince Friedrich Wilhelm and his second wife.

93
Princess Viktoria Luise of Prussia

Viktoria, born in 1982, is the only daughter of Prince Friedrich Willhelm's second marriage.

94

Prince Michael of Prussia

Prince Michael, born in 1940, is the second son of Grand Duchess Kira of Russia. He first married a commoner, Jutta Jörn but divorced her and is now married to Brigitte von Dallwitz.

95

Princess Micaela of Prussia

Micaela, born in 1967, is the elder daughter of Prince Michael and Jutta Jörn.

96

Princess Nataly of Prussia

Nataly, born in 1970, is the younger daughter of Prince Michael's first marriage.

97

Prince Georg Friedrich of Prussia

His Royal Highness Prince Georg Friedrich, born in 1976, is heir to the throne of Prussia. His father Prince Louis Ferdinand, who died in 1978, was the third son of Grand Duchess Kira.

98

Princess Cornelie-Cecile of Prussia

Her Royal Highness Princess Cornelie-Cecile, sister of Prince Georg Friedrich, was born in 1978 just after her father's death.

Prince Christian (2nd right) with parents and sister.